DECENCY

DECENCY

Charles S. Lauer

CORPORATE VICE PRESIDENT, CRAIN COMMUNICATIONS
PUBLISHING AND EDITORIAL DIRECTOR, MODERN HEALTHCARE

PUBLISHED BY SECOND RIVER HEALTHCARE PRESS
BOZEMAN, MONTANA

DECENCY

Second River Healthcare Press
20 B Shawnee Way
Bozeman, MT 59715-7624

(406) 586-8775 Phone
(406) 586-5672 FAX

info@SecondRiverHealthcare.com

Editor: Robert G. Goldsborough
Cover Design: Bruce R. Barnhart
Typesetting/Composition: InVision Communications

Lauer, Charles S., DECENCY / Charles S. Lauer

ISBN 0-9743860-2-2 (hard cover)   ISBN 0-9743860-3-0 (soft cover)

1. Health services administration. 2. Motivation. 3. Inspiration

Library of Congress Control Number: 2005935141

First Printing November 2005

DEDICATION:

To my daughter Kathleen, my son, Randy, and my wife, Maggie; plus my granddaughters DeDe and Emma; my grandsons Chuck, Ted, Tommy, Matt, Jack and Patrick. You will always be my loves.

ACKNOWLEDGMENTS:

I have always been struck by how decent people are all over the world. Wherever I travel both in and out of this nation I find people truly do care about each other. Too often, however, the honest and decent and honorable people are not recognized for their good deeds because what they do on a day-to-day basis doesn't make big headlines. But they are the ones who do make a difference in this country as well as others and make this world of ours a better place. I dedicate this book to them because they make life so enriching and worthwhile. I would like to especially acknowledge Cathy Fosco and Todd Sloane for their encouragement and support.

TABLE OF CONTENTS

FOREWORD

I decided to name my book *Decency* because I believe that there isn't nearly enough of it today. Too many people are too busy or distracted to practice habits drilled into them as children—respect for elders, opening doors for others, greeting them in passing, remembering to say thanks when they do something for you. The social respect that binds us to one another as a community has broken down. I know there are increasing numbers of people who may not have ever learned manners. Their parents may have been oblivious to others and passed down that trait to their children. But I witness educated people from good homes who are rude, uncaring and even cruel toward strangers and colleagues alike.

We all have an obligation to do what we can to restore civility and compassion in our society. It's a sign of strength, not vulnerability, to be decent to others. Yes, we all come from different economic, cultural, religious, ethnic and racial backgrounds. We have different outlooks on world affairs and national politics. We are of different generations, dress differently and listen to different music, but we share this street, this office, this community, this country. Our very differences should lead to respect for those around us, and make us more aware of what an interesting and complicated world we live in.

One of the barriers to decency is the speed at which everyone is living. We have so much to distract us that it's no wonder that so few people make eye contact or really listen to what the other person is saying. True communication is lost when everyone's attention is on what is to come next. Living in the moment is becoming harder and harder in an age of cell phones, PDAs, pagers and e-mail.

I attended a small college in Vermont called Middlebury many years ago. Back in the 1950s it was part of the school's tradition that everyone in the student body greet one another with a

"Hi." As a college student I thought to say "Hi" to complete strangers was a little silly but as I've grown older I realize how important it is to recognize one another as a fellow human being. I do this daily as I walk the streets of Chicago and when I'm traveling around the country. If you want to make a person smile, say hello to a stranger on the street. People enjoy others saying hello to them. It makes them feel just a little bit better in the moment. It connects people as human beings.

Decency also has to be something we practice in the workplace. This book comes from the thoughts I put down each week in my column in *Modern Healthcare* magazine. I have been proud to be associated with the healthcare world for more than three decades. People in healthcare are really very special. I've had the honor of having them as my friends and colleagues. Many are passionately devoted to the core mission of healthcare, caring for patients. Like the rest of the world, however, healthcare has experienced dramatic change. Competition has become more intense. In some cases, some hospitals are fighting for their very survival and in order to do that they have to employ some hardball tactics. Many are "right-sizing" and "downsizing," nice-sounding euphemisms for cutting people. Others are engaging in some pretty vicious competition in their markets.

The forces buffeting healthcare leaders include paying for an amazing array of new technologies, dealing with increasing government regulation, keeping bricks and mortar up to date, coping with a nursing shortage and placating physicians who are also worried about their economic future. Executives must do all of this at a time when Medicare and Medicaid reimbursement has failed to keep pace with costs, employers are cutting coverage and more uninsured people are turning up in emergency rooms. It's a tough environment and one that requires maturity and competent leadership skills on the part of healthcare managers.

The problem is that too often with all the emphasis that is placed on the business side of healthcare, the needs of patients are sometimes lost in the shuffle. What makes healthcare such a special industry is caring for people at their most vulnerable moments. When patients believe they are anything less than the center of the healthcare mission, something is very wrong. I submit that many patients have that feeling today.

I mentioned the relationship between hospitals and physicians, which has become one of the stickiest issues in healthcare. Recently the CEO of a major healthcare system contacted me to ask for my thoughts on that issue. Specifically he wanted to know how a provider could do a better job of working with referring physicians. I believe the answer is relatively simple. It involves communicating better with physicians. They should be part and parcel of all decisions that are made by the C-suite executives. Too often doctors have been left out in the cold and because of that they wind up opposing new initiatives by management. As too many CEOs have learned, that's a recipe for disaster. As a matter of fact, because of physician unrest many CEOs have lost their jobs. Physicians are no different than anyone else, they want to be treated with dignity and respect and that includes not only communicating with them but also seeking their advice on all matters that affect them.

Whether its physicians or loved ones, colleagues or friends, treating people well always brings dividends. I hope you enjoy *Decency*.

Preface

Decency: That which is proper or becoming; the quality of conforming to standards of propriety and morality; the quality of being polite and respectable; seemliness; hence, freedom from obscenity or indecorum; modesty.

These are among the dictionary definitions of DECENCY, the subject of Chuck Lauer's latest book. I can't argue with any of these, but somehow they are not enough. Decency is deeper than modesty ... or what is polite ... or what fits the standards of propriety. And Chuck Lauer understands that.

Decency is about doing the right thing and being a good person.

There are few people who have a better sense of doing the right thing than Chuck Lauer. In his Publisher's Letters in *Modern Healthcare*, Chuck has reminded us repeatedly what it means to be a good person. He doesn't talk about complicated theories of morality. Instead, he tells stories that demonstrate the qualities that lead toward a fuller life, stronger relationships, a better society.

Chuck Lauer wears his heart on his sleeve. In this book you will see that. With Chuck, what you see is what he really is, day to day, year after year—a man who cares about people, about doing the right thing, about his country and his family and friends, and about the healthcare industry where he has spent his career ... and about the Cubs.

This book weaves stories of these passions together into a quilt of reminders. The technique is the time-honored one of the storyteller. As he spins tales from his experiences and observations, he incorporates a lesson. And each lesson touches on an aspect of DECENCY. Some are the simple basics of decency such as what is polite. Some grow from the basic tenets of the world's great religions. Most will not be new to the reader. But pulled together, they form a pattern that can guide us to do the right thing.

By Diane Appleyard
President
Healthcare Research & Development Institute
Pensacola, FL

Chapter 1

WORK
PLACE

TEAMWORK NEEDS CULTIVATING

A sense of mission, the right training and a leader to follow are keys to success

People are any organization's most valuable assets, but for some reason we keep forgetting this simple point. Instead, we get caught up in the latest system that is going to make everything perfect and everyone more efficient and economical, ignoring the fact that it is people who make systems work.

I watched a television interview the other night with Jack Welch, the dynamic CEO who retired in 2001 from General Electric Co, where he did an absolutely miraculous job of turning the company around. Although his image later took a beating, that doesn't take away from the point that he used the team concept to perfection at GE. He proved that putting together a group of quality people who are loyal, committed and focused makes the team formula work in business. Conversely, if you have a bunch of talented but selfish people who won't work well with colleagues, you won't have a team whose sum will be greater than its parts.

The best example of this that I can think of is team sports, where you can, with a little knowledge of the game, watch how well a team performs. Of course, you have to have good athletes to succeed in sports such as football, hockey or basketball. Nobody wins without talent, but how many times have you seen top players end their careers without winning a championship? On the other hand, there are teams that didn't have overwhelming talent but made up for that with team chemistry and won titles. Too often the so-called superstars worry about their own statistics and awards and forget they need teammates to win the big games. Well, the same is true in business, where one individual, through either ego or ignorance, can throw a monkey wrench into the morale and productivity of any group. It happens too much and it's hard to correct.

That's where leadership comes into play. Good leaders understand that success depends on getting good people to work together toward common goals. Most successful companies not only spend a lot of time recruiting the right kind of staff, but they also make sure that once on board the new hires get the attention and training they need to succeed within the team concept.

There isn't a manager I have ever talked to who hasn't been willing to tell me about his or her superb training program. One CEO told me, "We leave nothing to chance. We drill our people constantly so they understand the significance of what it is they do." Now that is an admirable goal, and a lot of companies train their people thoroughly—at the beginning, that is. Later, when seasoned employees want to learn new skills, no new training is available because it's seen as too expensive.

Good people wouldn't stand for this type of treatment and often will leave a company because they are not being challenged or stimulated by their leaders. So what to do?

It's really pretty simple. To use that sports analogy again, start with a good game plan: How many people in any organization really understand the organization's mission? I'll guarantee you that too many companies lose their edge and market share because they don't remind their people of the shared goals and the plan to achieve them.

Each department and individual should know how they fit into the corporate plans. This takes a lot of work and there is some risk involved, especially if someone leaves your organization and tells a competitor what your plan is.

Years ago, there was an international airline that was a hair away from declaring bankruptcy. It hadn't shown a profit for many years and the red ink seemed to be getting worse all the time. The CEO was mediocre. He worried more about the inventory (airliners) and gate leases than the actual product, the quality of the flying experience. What he couldn't seem to understand was that for any business to survive and prosper it needs customers. That seems so rudimentary, but too often top execs are under so much pressure they forget what it is they are there to do, and that's to make intelligent decisions. Things had gotten so bad after a time that the board was called into emergency session to discuss the possibility of bankruptcy. The board was set to vote to seek bankruptcy protection, but one member of the board wouldn't let it happen. He persuaded the board to hire a young executive who had made incredible changes at a competing airline. Consequently the young CEO was brought in to save the day.

His first move was to bring all of his execs together and ask them what kind of business the airline was in. One executive raised his hand and blurted out, "The airline business." Everyone laughed, but the new CEO suggested what he meant was for his people to arrive at a consensus of what the particular mission of that airline should be. It took days for all the execs to arrive at a consensus, but during that time they got to know each other better and began to think of themselves as a team. Eventually a consensus was reached, which was "to take passengers from one location to another safely and on time."

And so executives of the airline fanned out all over the world to bring all the thousands of employees on board with the company's new mission. Along with the new mission statement, the new CEO introduced a new customer service program, and the airline soon became known for its coddling of passengers and its profitability.

Team play in business is not a new concept. But teams still need leaders, and too often that leadership is unfocused and weak. When quality people see this, they move on, leaving the company less and less effective, with failure a distinct possibility.

People need to be inspired day after day, month after month and year after year. It takes a sense of purpose and a lot of hard work, but isn't that what leaders are paid to do? It all comes down to people.

GET IN TOUCH, STAY IN TOUCH
Successful companies are those that know how to relate to their workers

Studies have been done on why employees seek to change companies. If they had to guess why this is, most people would probably surmise that the No. 1 reason people leave a company is the promise of more money. But if that were your guess, you would be wrong.

Exit interviews show that the top four reasons people leave an organization are: not being treated with dignity and respect; not being able to make an impact on the organization; not being listened to; and not being rewarded with more responsibility. Low pay is down the scale at five or even lower. The overriding theme of the workplace is that people want to be respected.

To make my point I'll relate a story from several years ago about the chief executive of one of this country's major airlines. When this fellow joined the company, his background was in the hotel industry where he had a track record as someone who could take losing properties and make them profitable. He was young and full of energy, and his people skills were legendary. Everyone respected him. No employee was too far down the ladder for his attention if he or she was having problems.

We lost contact for a couple of years, and then the next thing I knew he was named the president of the airline. I wasn't surprised, really, because he was such a gifted individual.

Later I would read glowing articles in magazines and newspapers about how talented he was. Pilots, flight attendants and mechanics had nothing but great things to say about him. Business schools used him as a classic example of how leaders should conduct themselves in dealing with employees. I was proud to know my friend was doing so well.

The airline did well for a number of years thereafter. On one flight I took on his airline, a flight attendant told me how wonderful my friend was because he talked with and listened to everyone. He would fly from coast to coast repeatedly, on each flight spending time with the employees. His popularity knew no bounds. Only a short time later, however, it became apparent something had happened. From time to time I would pick up a newspaper and read something about the airline unions being unhappy about the way they were being treated. I began to read critical articles about my friend having become aloof from his employees. Then, shortly after that, my friend retired, and now occasionally he does some consulting.

I was stunned when I read about how employees' views of him had changed so dramatically in such a short period of time. When I read he was seen as aloof, it sure didn't sound like the man I knew. So I began to ask around in the airline business about what had happened, and here's what I was told. My friend had become more and more engrossed in expanding the airline into other lines of business. In doing so he lost contact with the rank-and-file workers. He didn't have time to talk to them, to listen to them and to test their morale. Consequently, everyone from pilots to mechanics felt that they were being ignored, and that's when everything started to fall apart. Although this all happened years ago, the airline still has labor problems, and it has never fully recovered from the debacle.

So I have seen personally what can happen to a popular leader who forgot how to treat employees with dignity and respect. This leaves workers frustrated about not being able to have an impact on an organization, and that's how you lose good people. All of us, no matter what our rank, want to feel that what we do not only has an impact on our organization but gives us the recognition and rewards we deserve for our efforts. Any leader worth his or her salt understands this.

How can anyone feel important unless he or she is listened to? This is such a basic human need, and if we are listened to and treated well, we hope to be promoted into jobs with more responsibility in the same company.

But there are other important parts of making people feel respected that are so simple and yet somehow difficult for many bosses to comprehend. Too many leaders feel the best way to run a business is to micromanage everything and everybody. This thwarts workers' growth and can act as a cancer in the body of an organization. Micromanagers can be some of the most gifted people in the organization, but if they don't cede control over things and get out of the way, it works against employees' individual growth. It's as true today as it has been forever. We learn by our mistakes, and unless people are given the latitude to make mistakes, they don't grow, and the company is saddled with mediocre managers. In the end this can bring down an organization.

Trusting people, supporting them and letting them know how much you appreciate them goes a long way toward breeding confidence, boosting productivity and ensuring loyalty. This is why so many successful businesses have so little turnover. They try to make sure that gifted, enthusiastic people are promoted. Trying to entice someone away from a company like this is almost a lost cause. Treat others as you would like to be treated.

THE PERSONAL TOUCH
In any business, it can make all the difference

A conversation I had recently with an investment banker reminded me of something I always talk about with people I know in the healthcare industry, which is that managing people requires a personal touch. Literally.

Sometimes all of us use the phone or e-mail or fax machine as a more efficient means of keeping in touch with co-workers or clients. It certainly is more convenient, and you can keep working in your office on other things while getting your message across. There are days when schedules and time pressures mean that is all you can do. But even in this age when electronic communication is getting more and more advanced, face-to-face meetings are still invaluable. Nothing makes employees feel better than to have their boss stop by to let them know how important they are to the company's operations. Nothing makes customers more likely to want your product or service than having some sort of personal rapport with you.

With that in mind, let me relate a story the investment banker told me. He had just finished a trip to Las Vegas, where he had been attending an industry meeting. While he was there, he thought he should stop in at two companies based there. He had done some work for these companies and felt like he should at least say hello to the principals of the firms.

"I had never met these people before, but they never seemed to be bothered by the fact I hadn't called on them personally," he told me. "Still, I felt guilty I hadn't bothered to visit them. So when I finally got to see them they were most cordial and treated me royally. On top of it all they gave me some more business that I wasn't even expecting. I guess the old axiom is true, that nothing can take the place of a personal call."

You bet it's true. But in spite of this, many people in the business still don't understand the importance of a personal call on a client or potential customer. Evidently they don't know there simply isn't any substitute for looking someone in the eye, shaking hands with them and taking their measure. If nothing else, calling on someone you are doing business with is a sign of courtesy and respect.

But it actually goes much deeper than that. There have been studies done in the selling business that show that if other things such as quality and price are equal, a person will end up buying from someone they know best. It's simply human nature.

The same rule applies to the healthcare industry. I think about the many times I have been inside a healthcare institution—either on business or because I needed medical attention—and have mentioned the name of an executive I know there. Guess what? Quite often the person I was talking to had no idea whom I was talking about. That has always shocked me, for a variety of reasons. One is that if the top people are really involved in their institutions, the people who work in the trenches would certainly know who they were. I don't want to single out healthcare, by any means. I know that in many American corporations many of the middle managers or other workers have never met anyone from the top management team, and I believe it is rarer to find that in healthcare, which by its nature is a people business.

Whenever I hear employees say they have never met a senior manager, that to me is a terrible failure of leadership. All of us want to be appreciated, and there is nothing better than for a single individual or a group of individuals to hear from their leader as to how important what they are doing is to the company's success. It fosters a sense of teamwork, and without that, it's pretty hard to have much success.

Let me give you another example of the power of the personal touch: In the early 1980s, Scandinavian Airlines System, a major European carrier, was on the verge of declaring bankruptcy. The board was in a somber mood and puzzled about what to do. But one of the board members felt he had a solution to the problem and got the other board members to go along with him. The solution was hiring a man named Jan Carlzon away from British Airways, where he had a track record of success. Carlzon's predecessor at SAS had been preoccupied with keeping up the airline's inventory of planes and gate leases around the world. It didn't take Carlzon long to figure out what was wrong with this approach. He knew the company could have all the planes and gate assignments in the world, but if there weren't passengers filling the seats the airline wasn't going to make money. A program of superb customer service was instituted, which included planes leaving on time and arriving at their destinations on time. But as Carlzon took control he also did something else that made all the difference in the world. He and his executive team traveled all over the world to inform all 40,000 airline employees about the new plans. They asked each employee personally to buy into the plan and become a real member of the team. Carlzon's vision worked, and in very short order SAS became one of the top airlines in the industry.

What was true then is true today. Managers have to make themselves visible to the people who work for them.

I happen to know that many healthcare leaders wholeheartedly believe in this approach. They understand that visiting colleagues in person, not through a memo or videotape, makes all the difference in the world. But everyone needs to do this, no matter how large or diverse the organization you lead.

So if you want to make someone feel important, don't sit in the office shuffling papers and slurping coffee; get out as often as you can to visit even a few of the people who make your institution special. I guarantee it will not only improve their morale, it will also make you feel even better about being their leader. Communicate.

A GOOD ATTITUDE IS ESSENTIAL TO SUCCESS
Avoid envy, gossip and negativism

It seems to me that most of the people who succeed in life don't waste their time envying others. But that's only one of their strengths. What are some of the others? One is that they're positive. They love their lives and what they are doing. Furthermore, they avoid gossiping about their friends and colleagues. Maybe they would if they had time, but most successful people I know are too busy pursuing their dreams.

If you want to get ahead in any endeavor, an optimistic approach is key. Look around you. Look at the individuals who get promoted, who always seem to be where the action is and who seem to get things done without a lot of fuss. Is it just a matter of talent? Is it because they have an advanced degree? Is it because they are just plain lucky? What makes the difference? It's their disposition. Whom do you enjoy spending time with? People who are cynical and negative or those who always seem to have a good day, smile a lot and are filled with energy and enthusiasm? Successful individuals have a knack for listening to others and making them feel very special. Remember, success comes in many forms. People who always have an optimistic outlook are already successful because they're content with their lot in life and they're hopeful no matter what their circumstances.

An enemy of a positive attitude is envy. It eats people up. Having an envious spirit guarantees unhappiness. Looking over your shoulder all the time seeing how much others have or if colleagues are treated better than you or are making more money than you is simply a waste of energy. It's a tip-off about how small individuals can be. Envy gives birth to negativity. People become so caught up in the envy syndrome that they forget that the only way to attain excellence is to focus on their own goals and achievements, not those of others.

Gossip is also a tremendous waste of time and energy. Gossip usually involves taking other people's inventory, which in turn demeans those other people. Losers love to pull others down to their own miserable level. Since they aren't committed to anything and usually have negative attitudes, they are destined to fail and want others to fail with them. Walk away. Don't help others destroy reputations. Do something constructive with your time. There are simply too many exciting things to accomplish. Preoccupy yourself with them. The world is filled with opportunity.

It's never too late to make your mark, find your fortune or do whatever it is you want to do. So many people have accomplished incredible goals when others have simply given up. Yes, life is a struggle and is filled with all kinds of challenges, but the fun part is to take it on and make something happen that is positive and exciting. The late Karl Bays, who ran American Hospital Supply Co., made it so successful in the '60s, '70s and '80s, had a sign on his wall that read: "Spectators will kindly remove themselves from the playing field." Don't let gossip and envy turn you into a spectator. Get in the game with a great attitude and you'll usually win.

STICKING TO THE BASICS
Without them, any business is in trouble

How many times have I talked about the basics? You know, the essentials of success such as listening, manners and perseverance. They're so elementary, yet it's so easy to fall out of practice. I think we all need to be reminded now and then about the importance of getting back to the basics, and there's never a better time than at the dawn of a new year.

When people neglect the basics, it's often out of haste. We're a society that's always in a hurry, so we look for shortcuts. Another reason the basics get left behind is because the importance of fundamentals was never emphasized in the first place. Those offenders were probably never properly mentored. Another tenet here is that patience is a virtue. It's an integral part of getting things done properly and with high quality. But no matter how much we try or how much we've been advised to do otherwise, all of us at one time or another are in such a rush to get things done that we try to take the easy way out. That almost always undermines our effectiveness. In business, just like in sports, when the fundamentals are overlooked, the game gets sloppy.

I'm often reminded of the importance of sticking with the basics by the actions of people who call on me trying to sell something. When I see intelligent people do things they should know are inappropriate, I'm always surprised. One thing that's a no-no in sales is violating the personal space of someone you are trying to sell by reaching over the person's desk or standing almost on top of the person to show your materials. Other basics in sales include eye contact, a firm handshake, enthusiasm and commitment to your company and your customers. But they're often missing ingredients.

Leaders, especially in business, also need to remember their basics. For starters, it's imperative that they mentor their employees. Out of paranoia too many leaders seem unwilling to give of themselves and reveal their thoughts about how an organization can do a better job. However, if managers are to command respect from their colleagues, they need to be ready to jump in and offer guidance in the day-to-day challenges. Employees look to their leaders to set an example in the workplace. This is another situation in which listening is absolutely essential, by both managers and employees.

We're also operating in a new information age. Of course, the Internet is a major part of it. Though we should embrace the technology's potential, we still need to remember the basics of good communication. Talk about intruding into someone's personal space. How many e-mails do you receive in a given day? I'll bet most of them are unsolicited from people you don't know. We need to mind our manners in our contacts with others, whether it's via phone, fax or e-mail. When we become too casual, communication suffers.

I wonder how many of us have put together a plan for the new year. The first thing I always promise myself is to work harder and make more calls than I did last year. Furthermore, I realize that making money isn't a sin, and it's what selling is all about— making money by giving quality service. I know that the best way to do that is by outworking my competition, but today many individuals in and out of sales think that working hard means a 9-to-5 schedule. But if you truly want to succeed, the 9-to-5 routine doesn't even scratch the surface.

DRESSING THE PART
It's good business to avoid the casual look

During the past few years, I've noticed that people working the booths at trade shows seem to be dressing more casually than in previous times. Of course that's a reflection of what's been happening in the workplace. Casual has been in and formal has been out. As many of you know, I've never been a big fan of casual dress. To me, business attire is part of the package when it comes to professionalism. That's especially true in sales. I also realize that because someone wears a suit doesn't necessarily make that person any more competent or trustworthy than anyone else. But whether we like it or not, appearances do matter. When you meet someone for the first time, that initial impression can be critical.

Nowhere is that more true than at trade shows, where vendors display their products and services to customers and prospects, and obviously want to make the best impression they can. But often that's not the case. To put it more bluntly, the way some reps dress at many of the shows I've attended has become almost slovenly. And I'm sure that's not the image any company wants to project. When I do business with someone, I like to think I'm dealing with a person who is responsible and takes pride in his or her appearance. I know this is a matter of personal preference. Too many people, what a salesperson is wearing might not matter that much. But I think you'll find that more and more, people are on my side. The pendulum is swinging back toward a more traditional style in the business world.

Somebody recently sent me an article from the magazine *Meeting News* discussing some trends at trade shows. The article cites a survey conducted by the Incomm Center for Research and Sales Training indicating that dress-down days at trade shows are on their way out. In a 1998 survey, 86% of customers didn't have a problem with the casual dress of salespeople working the shows. However, just two years later, another survey found that only 45% of customers were pleased with the laid-back appearance of the salespeople.

The president of Incomm, Allen Konopacki, suggests that the attendees' attitudes have changed because what was once casual yet stylish has deteriorated to "crumpled and unkempt." It was almost an "anything goes" attitude on the part of some salespeople, and that turned off a lot of their customers. "At trade shows, the exhibit staff's appearance creates a message of credibility, trust and respect for customers," Konopacki says in the article. He cites General Electric Plastics of Pittsfield, Mass., as an example of positive change. The reps for that company apparently traded in their sweater vests and open-collared shirts for more traditional blue dress shirts, black slacks and polished leather shoes. They used brightly colored ties to add some flair to the look. According to the article, wherever GE exhibited, more than 81% of the visitors considered the GE staffers more professional and credible than those at other booths sporting a more casual look.

Even though all of this might give you the idea people crave a formal approach in attire, that isn't quite what the survey shows. The Incomm research indicates that most people don't want a total return to the unapproachable corporate look. Although customers say senior staff should wear formal suits, they want salespeople working the exhibits to stay away from being too formal and maintain a more-approachable appearance. Another factor here is the globalization of our economy. "Most companies now do business on a global basis, and our research found that international customers do not always accept casual attire," Konopacki says in the article. "As a result, American companies are being forced back into a conservative appearance."

The message here is simple: When dealing with customers, try your hardest to look sharp. It's what people want and expect. And it's what they remember. If you want people to accept you as the professional that you are, you must act the part and look the part. It's just good business.

Sound advice about writing e-mails

Remember to be clear, concise— and courteous

We're in what could be called an e-mail explosion. It's convenient, and hard to beat for speed of communication. But something is missing. Namely good manners, proper English usage and appropriateness of content. I would guess that the majority of us get a flood of e-mail daily, most of which we discard as fast as we can click the mouse. Something needs to be done about that. A good place to start is with that next e-mail you're about to send. Is it necessary? Would it just contribute to the stream of "junk" e-mail? Would a phone call be a better way to handle it?

Another part of this craze is that with just about any e-mail we receive that is truly important, we make a "hard copy." That's usually because we want to study the communication before we act on it or want to file a copy for safekeeping. My question, then, is why not start with a hard copy? Is it really that urgent that you can't send a written memo or even a letter?

I was reminded about all these issues when I recently received promotional materials for a book titled *Customer Service for Dummies.* One of the press releases carried the headline "Ten most common e-mail etiquette mistakes. Lack of e-mail etiquette could be ruining your image." Apparently this and a lot of other advice can be found in what the publishers boast is "the much awaited, expanded second edition containing all new content on e-mail and the Internet." The authors are Karen Leland and Keith Bailey, who founded the Sterling Consulting Group in 1986.

According to their profiles, Sterling was the first American consulting company to win a major contract for customer service training within the British government. Both authors have also worked with large companies like American Express, AT&T, Marriott Hotels and Sun Microsystems. Because of their customer-service expertise, IDG Books Worldwide contacted them to write a book on the topic. The result was *Customer Service for Dummies.*

So what are the most common e-mail mistakes according to the authors?

- Unclear subject line. The "title" for your e-mail should be clear, concise and neutral.
- Poor greeting or no greeting. The authors say none of us would write a letter or leave a voice mail message without at least a simple greeting. The same applies for e-mail.
- Using abbreviations not commonly used or understood. The authors say ASAP or FYI are OK, but others can be confusing. When in doubt, spell it out.
- Unnecessary "carbon copies" of the posting. In other words, don't CC people who don't need to get involved. There are plenty of stories of people who were CC'd on memos that cast them in an unfavorable light.
- Sloppy grammar, spelling and punctuation. Use spellcheckers and proofread all e-mail. Don't make readers wince.
- Using all CAPITAL letters to make a point. According to the authors, when you use all capital letters in a message you are throwing a "HISSY FIT." It's the written equivalent of shouting. Anger isn't productive.
- No closing or sign-off. The person who receives your e-mail will probably think you are rude. Always end your e-mail on a positive note—no matter what the content of the message, the authors say.
- E-mail that's difficult to read. Use paragraph marks and proper spacing. Make the format reader-friendly.
- Messages have an unfriendly tone. Don't be hostile or accusatory in your writing. You're likely to get a hostile response. Remember, sometimes sarcasm or humor doesn't come across in an e-mail. In short, watch your manners.

- Lack of a clear request. What is it you're trying to accomplish with your message? Include a specific question or a request. And make sure it's clear and concise.

We all make these kinds of mistakes. Effective communication involves good old-fashioned common sense and courtesy. So I applaud Leland and Bailey for their excellent timing. Their advice is just what a lot us need right now to do a better job of communicating with our customers, colleagues and friends. E-mail can be risky business. Politeness is the key.

Make your presentations brief
Value the time of your audience

Las Vegas isn't my favorite town, but from time to time I'm
asked to speak to various healthcare gatherings, so I have to travel
to Sin City out of necessity. On one occasion, I spoke to members of the American Academy of Medical Administrators at their
annual congress, and after my speech I headed directly for the
airport to catch a flight back to Chicago. By luck I was able to
upgrade to first class and was assigned a seat on the aisle. As people walked past, the seat next to me remained vacant, and I
began to think I wasn't going to have a seat mate. But almost as
the flight attendants were about to close the door, a tall gentleman sat down next to me. I really wasn't in the mood to talk to
anyone. I had been up since about 3:30 a.m. Chicago time and
was exhausted. But this fellow struck up a conversation, and he
seemed friendly enough. He told me he was a physician. When I
asked him about his specialty and where he practiced, he told me
he was an orthopedic surgeon and performed surgery at Rush
Presbyterian-St. Luke's Medical Center in Chicago, a well-
respected organization. He told me he had been in Las Vegas to
give a talk. He followed that up by telling me his name, Richard
Berger, and at that point I'm sure my jaw dropped. I had been
trying to get an appointment with Dr. Berger for some time, but
I couldn't get in to see him until early next year.

Why would I be so surprised, and why do I believe the man
up above had somehow interceded in my life? I have been limp-
ing more and more in recent weeks, the result of a worn-out
right hip that's a carry-over from many years of playing hockey.
Besides the pain, the most serious consequence of my bad hip is
the fact my golf game has suffered. So recently I have been shopping around for specialists who perform total hip replacements.
There's certainly no shortage of top-caliber surgeons in the
Chicago area, but recently I saw a news segment on a Dr. Berger
who had developed a less-invasive hip-replacement surgery. The
procedure supposedly involves less pain and a speedier recovery.

People have sent me articles about Dr. Berger and his new approach to hip surgery. So it was really something to find myself sitting next to the man who was pushing the envelope with this new procedure, someone who I had been trying to see for weeks. I told Dr. Berger what a privilege it was to meet him and, if he had the time, I would love to learn more about his new technique. As soon as I got those words out of my mouth, Dr. Berger had his laptop computer open and proceeded to show me what the procedure involves. He also included some testimonials from patients who had the surgery. The presentation was brief but still explained everything in detail. It was impressive. So impressive, in fact, that I arranged to have the good doctor give me a new hip.

It's funny how such coincidences occur. I was amazed by the presentation Dr. Berger was able to give at a moment's notice. He obviously knew his business cold, and it was also obvious he had worked on his presentation so that it would demonstrate what he does succinctly yet effectively. Most presentations fall far short of that mark. They're usually too long, too boring and leave too many questions unanswered. We can all learn something from Dr. Berger's presentation—never waste someone's time. It's such a precious commodity for all of us. Of course not everyone can be a pioneer in hip-replacement surgery, but everyone certainly can learn to make concise, informative presentations. That would ease a lot of pain for those who have to sit through them. It's just good manners.

Meeting mania
Are all those sessions really necessary?

I'm not a big believer in meetings. I'm asked to attend many, but I pick and choose so I don't waste time. In too many cases, they turn into bull sessions without any agenda. Attendees go back to their jobs no better off than they were before the meeting Sure, meetings can be seductive. It's fun sitting around with your colleagues drinking coffee or munching on doughnuts. We might think we're being constructive by getting together now and then to make sure everybody is on the same page. Of course, some meetings are essential. Senior management should gather to talk about sales strategies or the introduction of new products. But valuable meetings are the exception rather than the rule. Some new research seems to support my thesis.

Recently, network MCI Conferencing released a study titled "Meetings in America: A Study of Trends, Costs and Attitudes Toward Business Travel, Teleconferencing and Their Impact on Productivity." The study had two phases: A survey of 1,300 business professionals who participated in at least six meetings a month along with in-depth research about a subset of this group. In the second phase of research, 660 people who frequently attend meetings kept a two-week diary in which they recorded all their meeting activity and their attitudes about the meetings. The research was conducted by InfoCom, a division of NFO Research.

According to the study, the typical professional attends 60 meetings a month, and more than one-third of the meetings were rated unproductive. Jay Crookston, then vice president of U.S. sales at network MCI, said: "It's clear American businesses have a severe case of 'meeting mania.'" Of course, because of the company he works for, Crookston has just the solution: "With travel costs on the rise and the vast majority of business people under pressure to reduce those costs, MCI encourages companies to take a hard look at how they're meeting and consider more cost-effective alternatives such as audioconferencing or videoconferencing," Crookston said. "There's no replacement for the value of meeting face-to-face with a new or prospective client, but by the same token, by traveling less, business people can gain time with family—and that's irreplaceable as well."

There's a lot of truth to that, but if you're in sales, I'm still a great believer in getting into the field to call on customers. Nothing can ever replace the personal call. Just make sure each call is absolutely necessary.

The "Meetings in America" study also concluded that 46% of professionals are attending more meetings than they were a year ago, and only 8% are attending fewer meetings. About a quarter of the respondents look forward to business travel, and 21% dislike it. "Travel fans" are less likely than "travel foes" to have spouses and children. Business professionals also cite frustration encountered when flying. Their irritations include flight delays and cramped seating.

Some interesting differences are found when comparing responses by sex. For instance, men find it harder to be away from home. About 75% of men describe being away from the family on business travel as stressful, compared with 56% of women. Men have a greater preference for in-person meetings, while more women prefer conference calls.

Also, nine out of 10 people have daydreamed during a meeting, and four out of 10 admitted dozing off. More men than women (41% vs. 31%) say they have fallen asleep in meetings. Unless you're sleep deprived, those meetings don't sound very productive.

Those are only a few of the study's findings. It's just more evidence that meetings can be a big waste of time and money. With all of us trying to do more with less, maybe an occasional videoconference or conference call isn't such a bad idea. Just remember that those are "meetings" too. Be judicious in your planning and always think before you meet.

DARE TO DREAM

The entrepreneur is a risk-taker

I recently had a meeting with three individuals who have started a healthcare-related company. It was one of the most exciting meetings I've attended in some time. They really know what the entrepreneurial spirit is all about. There was a lot of laughter as my visitors recounted what it's like trying to get a new company off the ground. Of course the fun is tempered by the sacrifices involved in such endeavors. The sleepless nights, the stress of trying to get appointments, being laughed at by potential customers, the uncertainty of everything, including where your next dollar is going to come from. Not to mention the endless travel and the time away from family.

It obviously isn't for everybody. Those who have a high tolerance for risk and uncertainty are much different than the average person. Entrepreneurs are looking for the pot of gold at the end of the rainbow. They have dreams and want to make them come true. They want to create something, taking a simple idea and bringing it to fruition. Some shy away from the gamble and in many cases regret that decision for the rest of their lives. They will really never know whether they had the right stuff. You could call them the "woulda, coulda, shoulda" crowd.

Don't be a spectator watching the world go by. There's too much opportunity out there. That opportunity exists because there's such a vacuum when it comes to true customer service. Start-up companies that begin with a foundation of superior service are way ahead of the pack. Most customer service is so bad these days that anything out of the ordinary will make a lasting impression.

The personal touch will also score points with customers. Most conglomerates deal with customers by computer. The phones are answered by computer, forcing the callers to push buttons to get service. If they're lucky they'll eventually reach a live human being. Some executive sitting in a plush office playing the corporate game of politics will tell you how the world has changed and that computers and the Internet are key to doing business more efficiently and economically. Frankly, in some cases that executive would be right. Many Internet and high-tech companies manage to remain entrepreneurial and customer-oriented. But often as they become more successful they seem to worry more about their stock value and concentrate less on customers. Too many execs have forgotten to do one very important thing: They never ask their customers how much they value the personal touch.

Entrepreneurs also take a different approach to decision-making. Two of the gentlemen I met with left their former employer because after an incredible start with a small, tight-knit staff, the firm was bought by a larger company. Then all the baloney started. Departments and fiefdoms were created almost overnight. New policies were initiated to "keep things under control." Some of the most basic actions first required a meeting to take place so permission could be obtained. As one of my visitors put it, "Before, all we had to do was walk down the hall to get something done. That usually took five minutes. But after we were bought out, everything changed. Decisions sometimes took days or weeks, and in today's competitive climate you can't do business that way. It was sad to see what happened."

Of course there are never any guarantees a new venture will succeed. If you need a guarantee before starting out, don't even try. You lack the entrepreneurial spirit. The uncharted territory of starting a business enterprise takes perseverance and intestinal fortitude. It takes leaders who believe in their abilities and are willing to put everything on the line. The gentlemen I met in my office were of that ilk, and that's why I enjoyed talking with them so much. They're swashbuckler types filled with drive, daring to take on all challenges. I'm sure they're a little scared, but I'm also sure they're having the time of their lives. Believe in yourself.

Chapter 2

CUSTOMER SERVICE

SIMPLE WORDS CAN MAKE THE DIFFERENCE
Try using "Please," "Thank you" and "May I?" more often

They're magical words that can make all the difference in the world, but too many of us seem hesitant to use them. They can open doors. They can start meaningful relationships. They can make someone's day. And those are just some of the things a few well-chosen words can do. But something seems to have happened to us as we have gone about the business of day-to-day living. We've forgotten how to be civil with one another. Apparently we're in such a hurry that we forget how important it is to take the time to be decent human beings. I know, we are in the new millennium and it's a fast-paced world. But are we really all that busy?

I'm referring to words such as "thank you," "please," "may I" and "I'm sorry," which shouldn't be in such short supply in a civilized society. When I'm not traveling, I always have a cup of coffee and a roll at what could be termed a "greasy spoon" in my hometown before I head downtown to the office. It helps me to gear up for the rigors of the day. But what gets to me is how rude some people can be to the waitresses there. Seldom do I hear customers say "please" as they place their orders. Something like: "I'll have the ham and eggs, please." It's simply a nice touch and shows respect for someone who's willing to serve us. And it's good manners. But maybe we're getting away from that type of thinking. Maybe we want to be curt with one another. Maybe I'm just overreacting. No, I don't think so. I believe everyone deserves to be treated with dignity and respect. A simple "please" should be second nature. Do we really need to be reminded to be polite?

Consider the words "thank you." Why is it that so many of us have a hard time getting those words out of our mouths? It doesn't take that much effort. Yet managers forget to thank their employees. Those of us in business forget to thank our customers. Husbands and wives forget to thank each other. The same goes for friends and family. We take so much for granted.

Saying "thank you" shouldn't be a painful thing to do.

Are we too inhibited or have we just forgotten how to be pleasant with one another? Are we so busy and so important that we just don't see the need to honor others with simple courtesies? Words like "please" and "excuse me" are all about basic decency. And that's what being a good person and a good citizen are all about.

Try a few of these words on others just as an experiment. Try them when you need help from a stranger or assistance from a colleague. But make sure you mean it! Few people can resist someone who adds a sincere "please." Think about your own experiences when others treat you politely. They stand out simply because someone has taken the time to be considerate. Successful salespeople know all about the power of good manners. Without employing them they wouldn't have gotten to first base in their careers. In many cases it separates winners from losers.

If you're not doing so already, make a habit of using some of these important words that can make a person's day. Say them often and see how well they work.

STICK WITH THE BASICS
Beware of management fads

I'm sure we've all heard the saying, "Give me a break, will ya?" That saying could apply to the new management tools that have come on the market in the past few years with promises to make companies more successful.

Not surprisingly, most don't deliver on those promises.

Consulting firm Bain & Co. put the spotlight on management fads and trends. Bain director Darrell Rigby, writing in *The Wall Street Journal* in 2001, recounted some of the recent experimentation with these new concepts. Some have achieved mixed results, while others have led to nothing but grief. The new management fads may look good on paper, but when someone tries to put these tools to work, they just don't jell.

Rigby noted that more than 10,000 business books had been published in a three-year period, many touting management tools that claim to "make their users incredibly successful by showing them new ways of doing business." Rigby hasn't been fooled, however, by all the glitz and glitter.

He used computer maker Gateway as an example of a company that threw itself into a series of management fads. In 1999, Gateway ranked No. 1 in revenue in the U.S. market for personal computers. Furthermore, the company didn't show any signs of weakness, even during the technology slump.

Management experts attributed Gateway's success to a number of management tools, Rigby said. One was termed "market disruption analysis." Here the senior executives of Gateway foresaw PC's going the way of pagers—slow growth, unacceptable margins. "Corporate venturing" came next. Gateway created a venture-capital arm to invest in new, diversifying businesses. The investment portfolio grew to $1.5 billion in a short period of time. Then came "customer relationship management." Gateway wanted to have lifelong relationships with customers. It expanded its product variety, spent hundreds of millions of dollars on more than 300 retail outlets and allowed customers to buy products on an installment plan.

What happened? Rigby wrote that Gateway had significantly missed its forecast, fired its chief executive officer, sharply reduced product options and announced a layoff of 3,000 workers. The stock price fell to $15 from $50. As a footnote to all of this, Gateway's co-founder reclaimed his old job as the top executive and has set about restoring profitability in its traditional computer products.

But Gateway is only a single example of companies that get carried away with management fads. We all know examples of companies that have gone down this path with disastrous results. The significance of Bain's involvement is that the firm during the past eight years has surveyed 5,600 senior executives from around the world seeking their opinions on management tools. Some 72% believed it is important to stay up-to-date on these tools, but 81% said most of them don't deliver on their promises.

One tool that executives considered the most effective in running their companies was the tried-and-true strategic planning. Other basics, according to Rigby, include mission and vision statements, along with pay for performance.

It comes down to one thing we've all been taught but usually forget until times get tough: Keep it simple. Stay with the basics and win; stray from your core business and fail. Experience is a great teacher.

SERVICE WITH A SMILE
A little friendliness can make all the difference to a patient...
...and the hospital

Sometimes someone helps you through a difficult situation and in the process turns it into a positive experience. A woman named Sharon Brooks did that for me. I was at Rush-Presbyterian-St. Luke's Medical Center in Chicago, having blood drawn for upcoming hip replacement surgery. It was the first of two trips for the same purpose, and I have to admit I was a little nervous. Prior to giving blood I had to register at the admitting desk. Usually when I go through that bureaucratic process I wind up offended. Maybe it's the impersonal manner in which I am treated. Often there is little eye contact, and no reassuring smile or other personal contact at a time when you could use it.

But at Rush-Presbyterian, Sharon not only smiled, she took care of me. She gave me strips of stickers that say "Smiles are Contagious—Catch One!" She was so full of energy, enthusiasm and goodwill I couldn't help noticing.

But that was only the beginning. After she got all the information she needed, she got out a machine that blew soap bubbles. Everyone in the admitting area was smiling, even those who were clearly there for something far more serious. Whatever the hospital pays Sharon, it isn't enough. She has probably done more for the image of the hospital than any expensive advertising campaign could do.

Now I guess some people might say that Sharon is a minor cog in the hospital's operation, but I don't buy that. The people who study customer service call my interaction with her a "moment of truth." That's when an individual first comes into contact with an organization, whether it is a pizza parlor, a physician's office or a Fortune 500 company. The way you are treated at that moment is usually the impression you have of that organization until someone takes a great deal of effort to change it. If you are treated rudely, you're turned off by that business.

The irony is that the person who greets you in any company

probably is going to be one of the lowest-paid individuals on staff, yet what they do and how they say it can make all the difference in the world to the success of any business. How many times have you called a business and been treated rudely by a person who immediately puts you on hold? How many times have you called some organization and never even got to a live person, and instead are sent from one extension to another in voice mail? Think of running a business where a customer who wants to spend money is either told to wait their turn or is asked to manipulate some buttons to get to the right person. Give me a break.

People are what make a business successful, and I don't mean the CEO—I mean the people who work on the front lines of the business. One of the legendary stories about customer service has to do with a doorman at the Four Seasons Hotel in Toronto. A harried lawyer rushed out of the hotel one morning and asked the doorman, Roy Dyment, to hail him a cab. Off the lawyer went to the airport, where he caught a plane back to Washington.

Not long afterward, the doorman looked down at the curb and was embarrassed to find he had failed to load the lawyer's briefcase in the cab. He felt terrible and called the lawyer's office in Washington. He reached a secretary, who asked Dyment to find a messenger service to get the briefcase from Toronto to Washington as soon as possible because the briefcase contained some documents her boss needed for an important meeting the next morning.

After promising to comply, Dyment asked the bell captain to cover for him the rest of the day, went to the airport and bought a round-trip ticket to Washington. When he delivered the briefcase to the stunned lawyer, Dyment merely apologized for any inconvenience he had caused and returned to Toronto.

The wonderful ending to that story is that Isadore Sharp, who at that time was the chief of the Four Seasons chain, was so impressed with Dyment's efforts that he made him the employee of the month and then later the employee of the year. Sharp understood what that act meant in terms of a quality customer service attitude.

Healthcare customers are no different from anyone else. They want to be treated with dignity and respect and a caring attitude. But too often in many healthcare facilities the customer/patient is greeted curtly and even ignored. That has gone on for far too long. When the boss cares and is willing to commit to quality customer service everyone benefits, including patients and employees. And the companies wind up on top while those that fail to inculcate the values of customer service usually fail.

So here's to you, Sharon Brooks, for reminding me of the importance of good customer service. Start with a smile.

Stressing service

Commitment to excellence comes from the top

I always find it exciting when a company takes a literal approach to customer service. I'd like to share a tale of two auto dealerships that illustrates what a difference a customer-friendly attitude can make.

A few weeks ago, while I was backing out of a parking garage near my office in downtown Chicago, I knocked the glass out of the rear-view mirror on the left side of my Chevrolet Suburban. It was a stupid mistake because I was in too much of a hurry and not paying attention. For safety reasons, I knew I needed to get the mirror fixed as soon as possible. I leased my truck from a dealer that's about an hour's drive from Chicago. However, thinking I could avoid the long trip, I called a dealer closer to my home in the northern suburbs. The service manager there told me to bring the truck in so he could see the extent of the damage. But he said he would probably have to order a new mirror because the dealership didn't have any in stock. It sounded like the process could take a week or so.

My next move was to call my dealer. I called the service department manager and told him about my problem. He immediately said there would be someone to meet me the next day at 9 a.m. in front of my office building. "I'll have someone bring a car up for you, and he'll pick up your truck. We'll fix it and get it back to you by the afternoon. Is that OK?" I told him that would be great. The next morning the driver was waiting for me with a loaner car. Later that afternoon my truck was returned with the mirror repaired. While we were switching vehicles, I asked the fellow from the dealership how often he did this sort of thing. "They have me driving all over the state every day taking cars to and from customers whose cars need repair or servicing," he told me. How's that for customer service?

The dealer I lease from is successful and well-known throughout Illinois. Even though it's farther from my house, I chose that dealership because I had heard nice things about the way the employees treat their customers. I had done business with the dealer close to home, but every time I needed some service the people there seemed more concerned about their schedule and system than taking care of my needs within a reasonable amount of time. Their service is probably no worse than average for the typical auto dealership, but is that really how you would want your business to be defined?

The difference in attitude and commitment is amazing. It's the difference between success and failure. Quality customer service is essential to any organization that wants to be successful in the long run. Too many healthcare facilities talk a good game when it comes to customer service, but in most cases they're still only offering lip service. Executives and clinicians still display too much arrogance. That's what turns patients and their families off and why so many people harbor ill feelings for the healthcare industry. So many of us seem willing to put up with service that's mediocre at best, which only perpetuates the problem.

Sure there are impossible customers. Some people are absolutely unreasonable in what they demand, but what most customers want is simply to be treated with a modicum of fairness and respect. They don't expect companies to run up the flag every time they step through the door, but they do like to know someone is listening and that they'll get satisfactory service in return for their money. Do those things and you'll win 99% of the time. But that commitment has to come from the person who runs the joint. Without that endorsement, customer service is simply an afterthought, and what customers usually get is something short of true "service." Avoid being average.

Customer service comes from the top
Chief executives need to show the way

Anyone who has read my columns over the years knows that I enjoy telling customer service stories as well as sharing examples of standout leadership. But it's becoming harder and harder to find examples of good service these days. The lack of customer service has almost become laughable. It really doesn't matter what industry you're in. The script is basically the same—stupid oversights by people who are poorly trained or don't really care what kind of service they deliver.

One particular incident was told to me recently by a fellow passenger on an early morning flight to Detroit from Chicago. As I was boarding, I noticed a gentleman with his right arm in a sling struggling to get his suitcase in the compartment over his seat When I asked him if I could help, he welcomed my assistance. Then he told me something that had happened to him the previous day. Here's what he told me: "I was boarding a flight yesterday to come to Chicago and was having a hard time getting my bag in the overhead compartment, so I asked one of the stewards if he could help me. He was reluctant to do so and mumbled something about workman's comp. He just stood there while I put my own bags in the bin. I couldn't believe it, especially from that particular airline, which keeps telling people in their ads how much their customer service has improved. Somebody better get into the field and check things out!"

The airline industry certainly isn't the only one guilty of providing poor service. In fact, a few carriers have won awards for their customer service. But name any industry and I can probably share horror stories of my own or others I've heard secondhand. What about healthcare? There's lots of room for improvement. A friend of mine recently had hip replacement surgery. Sometimes we have coffee together in a local eatery in my hometown. I hadn't seen this fellow for some time, but about three weeks after his surgery he came into the cafe and we had a nice chat. When I asked him about his surgery, he said his physical therapist told him he was doing well and would be back to normal in no time. However, something was bothering him. He made a point of telling me he hadn't seen the surgeon who performed the hip replacement since the day of the procedure.

Furthermore, in the hospital he was amazed at the lack of competent, consistent nursing care. He told me he never saw the same nurse twice. Maybe all of this is routine, but it's hard for me to understand why any surgeon wouldn't want to know firsthand how one of his patients was progressing, especially after a major procedure such as a hip replacement.

Something I've learned over the years is that superior customer service doesn't happen automatically for most organizations. It comes from the top. The chief executive has to be committed to a basic philosophy that puts the customers' needs first. And everyone has to be committed to that philosophy. The needs of employees also must be a high priority. After all, they're the ones on the front lines. I recently met an executive who truly has his priorities straight.

I traveled to Canada to attend a business meeting. As chairman-elect of a trade group in the information systems industry I had attended one of the organization's board meetings outside of Montreal. The meeting lasted two intense days, and those of us on the board got to know each other quite well. One of the members has a very successful software company and is respected throughout the IT industry. I was talking to another board member about this executive and asked what kind of a person he was. Here's how she described him:

"He is one of the most thoughtful and considerate people I know. Just this morning I saw him do something for one of his people that showed me how much he thinks of others, especially his colleagues. It was a small thing really, but it made a big impression on me. While we were all waiting to get on the plane, he went up to one of his people and insisted she take his first-class seat for the trip to Canada. He took her seat in coach. That's the kind of person he is."

What a great gesture. True leaders know how to make someone feel special and appreciated. It comes naturally.

Customer service and leadership have a lot in common, because they both involve treating people well. That philosophy will never go out of style. Humility is a winner.

RULE NO. 1: CUSTOMERS COME FIRST . . .

. . . And 10 other ideas that separate the winners from the losers in business.

In 1976, when Crain Communications purchased *Modern Healthcare* from McGraw-Hill, I used to call on a client in Cincinnati, American Laundry Co. The company once had advertised heavily in the magazine but had taken its advertising and switched to one of our competitors. I worked on that account for two years before the company finally returned to *Modern Healthcare* as a customer.

But I still can remember vividly the day I made my first call on American Laundry, whose offices were located at the top of a long, steep wooden staircase. I recall thinking that a visit to this company must have been a real chore for anyone who wasn't in good shape. After making it to the top of the stairs, I was met by a friendly receptionist who greeted me with a big smile and politely asked me to wait for a few minutes because the person I wanted to see was busy in a meeting.

That's when I noticed the sign behind the receptionist. It was a scroll from the Martinizing dry-cleaning company with some of the most inspirational words I had ever seen. In those days, Martinizing stores provided one-hour service. The sentiments on that scroll are the very thoughts that professional salespeople feel deeply about, but this was the first time I had seen those words presented in such an inspirational way. They are words to live by for anyone in business.

The words I want to share with you must be inculcated into the core beliefs of any business enterprise. Though most of us practice the spirit of these sentiments from time to time, they have to be taught and discussed consistently and openly among colleagues. They are what separate the winners and the losers in any enterprise, and they are simple steps to follow. I'll try to explain them from my point of view.

The scroll contained 11 vitally important points, and I'll start with the first: "A customer is the most important person in any business." Look around today and see what's happening. Many companies don't seem to realize that satisfied customers are the key to success.

For instance, while shopping at a Best Buy store in a Chicago suburb, I found myself in a long, slow line of fellow customers waiting to pay for their purchases. It surprised me that the line was so long and that the store had not made provisions for more salesclerks to handle traffic at the checkout stations. Suddenly, there was a burst of activity, and someone yelled, "Next in line, please." The long line quickly disappeared, and soon I was paying for my purchases. The young man at the checkout station apologized for the wait and added, "This is the third store they have sent me to straighten out. I have to institute some new policies that will make the place better for the customers. I've got to make everybody understand that customers come first."

This young man is going places.

The second thought on the scroll was, "A customer is not dependent on us. We are dependent on him." No. 3 read, "A customer is not an interruption of our work. He is the purpose of it." How many times have we heard someone say things such as, "If it wasn't for the patients, this would be a great place to work"? I've heard it, and I'll bet you have, too.

No. 4: "A customer does us a favor when he calls. We are not doing him a favor by serving him." I have done business with all kinds of service people who seem to feel they are doing me the biggest favor in the world by either serving me a meal or taking my money after I've purchased groceries or filled up with gas at a service station. Usually, there's no smile and very little eye contact, if any at all.

No. 5: "A customer is a part of our business, not an outsider." Too many businesses make this mistake constantly. They think of the customer as either an inconvenience or the enemy—and not the individual most responsible for the business being a success. Then there's No. 6: "A customer is not a cold statistic. He is a flesh-and-blood human being with feelings and emotions like our own."

Ladies and gentlemen, we are all customers, and we all

want to be treated with dignity and respect, especially when we are spending our money with a certain business. It's the least we should expect.

Yet in many cases, our first contact with a business is a computerized answering service, which instructs us what we must do to spend our money. Think about that.

The airlines are the worst offenders, and they continue to have financial woes. Years ago, I was stranded in St. Louis after my flight from New York was rerouted when O'Hare Airport was closed by inclement weather. I had a meeting the next morning in Chicago, and I was uptight about getting back. I telephoned Major Airline A and was greeted by a computerized voice-mail system asking me to press No. 1, 2, 3 or 4 on the telephone. And when I pressed 1, I waited and waited and finally gave up.

The same thing happened with Major Airline B. After another long wait on hold, I called Southwest Airlines. I was greeted by a real, live person right off the bat—even though it was 2 a.m. she cheerfully arranged to have a ticket waiting for me on a 6 a.m. flight to Chicago. I made my meeting. What impressed me most was not only the live greeting but the personal interest this woman took in my needs. She really seemed to care. It's no wonder Southwest is still making money when other airlines are asking Uncle Sam to bail them out of their financial predicament.

The seventh saying on that scroll was: "A customer is not someone to argue or match wits with." No. 8: "A customer is a person who brings us his wants. It is our job to fill those wants." No. 9: "A customer is deserving of the most courteous and attentive treatment we can give him." No. 10 is my favorite: "A customer is the lifeblood of this and every other business." That's really the bottom line, isn't it? Without customers, nothing happens. And finally, No. 11: "A customer is the person who makes it possible to pay our salaries."

These are 11 simple, basic statements that define the word customer. Nothing fancy, nothing dramatic and nothing very complicated. Yet most so-called "customer service" today literally stinks because people haven't been educated and trained to comprehend the importance of a customer.

DON'T OVERLOOK THE CUSTOMERS
They're the reason we are in business

Everything should start with the customer. It only makes sense since customers are really the only reason any organization exists. Yet if I were to ask a number of people in any company why they are in business, I'll bet you the customer would rarely get mentioned. Staff meetings, organizational meetings, product meetings, planning meetings and marketing meetings probably take up a good chunk of a given work week. But how often have you heard of a customer meeting? Everything we do on a day-to-day basis should have the customer in mind. Why is it we develop systems for our own convenience, but not for our customers?

One of my pet peeves I've used as an example before is the automatic answering devices encountered whenever you call companies to place an order, make reservations or ask for information. They're now installed in just about every place of business, but I think they only treat customers rudely and are an obstacle to good service. I don't know about you, but I'm tired of hearing: "All of our service representatives are currently busy serving other customers. But if you'll stay on the line, someone will help you shortly." Remember, the reason we are on the line is to give somebody an order and hand over our money. Yet here we are being greeted by an answering device telling us to push some buttons and then sit and wait. Companies need to wake up and get their priorities straight.

The first thought we should have when we come to work is how we can do a better job for the customer. Will that series of meetings benefit the customer? Will that new telecommunications system make it easier for the customer to do business with us? Do our new offices make us more efficient so we can better serve our customers? It's all so basic, but most of the time customers are treated like an afterthought.

The year just started, but I'll bet many of us haven't even given a thought about how we can improve the way we treat our precious customers. I'll even bet our customers were the last thing on our minds as we celebrated the holidays. Yet without our customers maybe we wouldn't have been able to give our loved ones the gifts we did. How many of us have gotten on the phone in the past couple of weeks to wish our customers a happy new year? How many of us have told those customers how much a part of our lives they are and how much we appreciate their business? Customers are just like you and me. They like to be told how important they are and how much we appreciate them.

Poor customer service and taking business for granted are problems that touch all sectors of the economy. Healthcare certainly isn't exempt. I see it all the time, but from year to year nothing really changes. Customer service in all industries is generally so bad that if a company treats customers with a modicum of service, it is heralded as a service giant. Yet that company is only doing what should be a given—providing good service to its customers.

How about treating this year differently. If someone wants you to attend a meeting, ask if it will benefit the customer. If it won't, don't attend. The same should apply for every other decision being made. If it's not good for the customer, don't do it. Measure every action with the customer-service yardstick. You'll be surprised how little you thought about the customer before.

By the way, if you do treat your customers well, the word usually gets around, and you'll end up with more business than you can possibly handle. Wouldn't that be a nice problem to have? Try something new.

Value your customer
It will pay off many times over

I belong to a dog-owners group. About eight of us bring our pets to a fenced-in area in a suburb of Chicago and let our dogs play together for about an hour early each morning. While the dogs are off having fun, we talk about a variety of subjects. One morning recently the topic was airline customer service. Most of us in the group travel a lot on business. One in particular, the chief executive officer of a marketing firm, travels extensively overseas. She was angry about the way she was treated on a trip recently on one of the major U.S. airlines. She said she was so upset that she sat down and wrote a 12-page letter to the airline's CEO.

She made it plain to us that she was disgusted with the service she received for the money she paid. She eventually received an apologetic form letter from the airline, along with a gift certificate, but none of her complaints was addressed. She vowed to do everything possible to avoid flying that airline again. This executive travels frequently in Europe and the Far East—big-ticket fares that airlines should go out of their way to protect. But because some employees weren't on the ball, that carrier has lost a valuable customer.

Communication Briefings, published by Capitol Publications in Alexandria, Va., once ran an article titled "Some Customer Service Math," which the executives of that airline should read thoroughly. Included are the "Top 10 Service Commandments" from the International Customer Service Association in Chicago. The First Commandment states: "Cultivate an obsession with the customer, because your organization is in customers' hands. Math: A 5% increase in customer retention equals between 25% and 80% increase in profit, according to a Harvard Business School study." That's a startling statistic, but there's lots more.

Commandment No. 2: "Be committed from the top down. Math: Some 95% of business owners give themselves a nine for customer service on a one-to-10 scale. But most of their customers wouldn't rate them anywhere near that."

Commandment No. 3: "Make a customer, not a sale. Math: Organizations that emphasize customer service see 12 times the return on sales as those that put a low priority on service."

Commandment No. 4: "Exceed customer expectations. Math: Increasing your customer retention rate by 2% has the same effect on profits as cutting costs 10%."

Commandment No. 5: "Keep your word, whether you say it in person, over the phone or in an ad. Math: If customers walk away unhappy, 87% will tell nine or 10 others about the poor treatment. And the remaining 13% will spread the bad news to 20 others."

Commandment No. 6: "Have patience. No matter how busy you are, customers are why you're in business. Math: Lack of attention from front-line employees accounted for 70% of lost customers, one study said."

The final four—"Provide solutions and good feelings by looking at every complaint as an opportunity; say thank you; encourage customer feedback; and recognize customer service excellence"—offer even more enlightening statistics. For instance, "it costs five to 10 times more to get a new customer than to keep the ones you already have; more than two-thirds of customers who leave do so because they perceive indifference to them; 68% of customers who stop doing business with a company do so because of poor service."

There's plenty of data showing the importance of good customer service, no matter what business you're in. And the healthcare industry certainly isn't exempt. It pays off time and again, but it requires total commitment, training, follow-through and hard work—every day. Answer each letter properly.

KEEP IT SIMPLE: GIVE GOOD SERVICE

*Author tells us the basic ingredients of companies' recipes
for sustained success*

Anyone who has read my columns over the years knows that I love quality customer service. All of us have seen really first-rate service, and when you experience how wonderful it is, you also marvel at how simple it is. It really doesn't take a genius to figure out what makes for good service, but too often we are moving so fast we don't always take note of it.

Here's how simple it is: Any company, large or small, is in the business of serving customers. Without customers, any business, no matter how sophisticated or unusual its product, will fail. So if you don't serve your customers, you lose them. Now that shouldn't be too difficult to figure out. So why is it you run into bad service almost everywhere you turn, from the local gas station to the airlines and, yes, the healthcare delivery system?

We have become a nation that is so grateful for even a modicum of service at almost any business establishment that someone who offers good customer service can enter almost any market and be successful right off the bat. It's also why some businesses stick around in difficult markets when their competitors all fall away.

I have read a delightful book on this topic by Leonard Berry, a professor of marketing and founder of the Center of Retailing Studies at Texas A&M University. The 1999 book, *Discovering the Soul of Service: The Nine Drivers of Sustainable Business Success,* was a page-turner for me. It is a well-researched, enlightened and focused look at customer service from a different perspective. Berry had written me a few weeks before about his faculty-development leave at Mayo Clinic, and I had quoted him in a column I wrote talking about the healthcare industry's need to refocus its mission and vision.

Berry's work is filled with common sense information about how 14 very different companies were able to sustain customer acceptance and financial success. Although the firms are quite different in field, size and structure, they are quite similar in their unending quest for constantly improving the way they take care of their customers.

Berry did his homework in choosing companies that met his criteria for offering sustainable success. He makes it clear that the purpose of his book is to identify, describe and illustrate "the underlying drivers of sustainable success in service businesses." Berry visited each company he chose and interviewed senior and middle management. He also followed up with numerous phone calls. On top of this he personally experienced service delivery at the sample firms, collected a small mountain of material from them and conducted secondary research on service management. In other words, he did his due diligence on these companies.

The companies he chose are for the most part little known nationally but they should be. One of the firms is Bergstrom Hotels, a group of three hotels in northeastern Wisconsin. According to Berry, the hotels have built a strong relationship with employees, customers and their communities through attention to detail, caring and a big corporate heart. The company was awarded the Wisconsin Service Business of the Year Award.

Another one is Midwest Express Airlines, which traces its roots to Kimberly-Clark Corp. Now an independent public company, Midwest Express takes great pride in offering "the best care in the air." In Zagat's 1997 survey of 60 of the world's largest airlines for comfort, service, timeliness and food, Midwest Express ranked first in the U.S. and was the only U.S. airline to place in the world's top 10. Other companies studied by Berry included the St. Paul Saints minor league baseball team, Enterprise Rent-A-Car Co., Dial-A-Mattress and Ukrop's Super Markets.

What the success of all these companies comes down to is picking the right people, training them in the culture of the company, treating customers and employees with respect and listening to their concerns, and paying attention to detail. It's all basic stuff, and all of the companies Berry tracks practice what they preach day in and day out. They don't skip anything. They make sure things are done right the first time and they make sure that all employees know their roles. The important thing that comes through, however, is that from the very beginning the companies that Berry highlights take the time to not only compete for the right employees, but don't rush into hiring people without first making sure the people coming aboard fit the culture. Too many times many companies hire people without taking the proper time to get to know how those potential employees feel about work and interacting with colleagues and customers. Haste, as they say, can mean waste and disaster.

Berry also believes that effective leaders can articulate their dreams and motivate others with their vision. He states, "Values-driven leaders continually convey by their words and actions the meaning of success. They not only make palpable the dream (where are we going, why are we going there), they define the indicators of progress (how we know we are getting there). A key factor in sustaining success is combining a compelling dream that inspires commitment with a success definition that is reinforcing rather than contradicting."

In short, what Berry is suggesting is that truly successful leaders lead by example; they don't mind getting their hands dirty doing the things that are necessary to help their colleagues deliver quality service. They don't hide in the executive offices shielding themselves from the day-to-day operations of their companies. A company's culture, its dedication to customer service, employees and colleagues, comes from the very top. Most great business success stories happen because those who lead truly believe in the mission and do everything they can to make it work. Service is job one.

THE WAITING GAME
You will lose business if you make your customers play it

One of the major frustrations for any of us is having to wait. For instance, we have all heard complaints such as, "I sat in that doctor's office for nearly an hour before she saw me. It was awful and I had to cancel two other appointments because I was running so late." Then there's waiting for someone to call you back or for a plumber or electrician to fix something in your home. Or the wait in line for a sporting event or to buy tickets to something you then have to wait in another line to actually get into.

In the military they call it, "Hurry up and wait." There are lines for everything, including eating. I remember well being processed through Camp Drake in Yokohama, Japan, during the Korean conflict and being rousted out of bed at 2 a.m. to get in line for breakfast, which didn't start until 5 a.m. Now that was a long line.

How many times have you walked into a store and looked for someone to wait on you, with nobody in sight? If you are lucky you eventually run into someone who might give you service, but you could wind up never being served.

It seems that these days people are more pressed for time, or at least we feel that way. We have a culture of instant gratification. We hate waiting for anything. We want things faster and quicker, and if we don't get it quickly, we move on to another vendor or restaurant or plumber or real estate company. We want service and we want it now.

Of course, nothing gets people as upset as traffic tie-ups, which cause road rage. It's no wonder that is so prevalent in large urban areas. Not only are people in more of a hurry, but congestion is much worse because there are more of us in the sprawling cities, and the urban infrastructure hasn't kept up with the growth.

Lately I have been hearing about something different, called "register rage." That's when people have to stand in line at the checkout counter and the line moves too slowly. People explode because they are so stressed or they have someone waiting for them or they are just plain tired.

Surprisingly, many businesses don't understand this, and they don't get it when their business starts falling off. You would think that communicating with your customers would be standard business practice, but it isn't always so.

The fact is, many corporate executives don't understand people's need to be treated promptly and considerately. Look around you at successful companies or individuals and you hear things such as, "He always returns your phone calls in a few minutes," or "Those people really believe in service. I called them that morning and they told me they would come out to the house by 2 p.m. and they actually showed up on time. It was terrific and they actually fixed the refrigerator in no time at all."

Why is it so many of us in our workplaces wait so long to answer phones? If you're on another call that's one thing, but why the hesitation to answer a phone and either take an order or give someone advice about something they bought at your business? Any phone should be answered after only one or two rings. Plus, there is no excuse for not returning phone calls. Business is business, and unless we understand that people don't like to be kept waiting, we are missing something crucial to success.

And that brings me to healthcare and all the waiting we do as patients.

I have just returned from a luncheon with a couple who are about to be married. They are young and very much in love and fun to be with. In the course of our luncheon, the future bride related a story about visiting a physician a day or two before. It was a routine matter but she was kept waiting for more than two hours, and this young, beautiful lady had the face of an ogre as she told the story of how long she had to wait for a five-minute visit with the doctor. She made it clear she has had it with that physician.

The same thing seems to happen with some regularity when any of us go to hospitals for various tests and, of course, the wait in physicians' offices is something we have all come to expect. I understand that sometimes things get backed up, but when it happens all the time it doesn't make a good impression on patients, who are the customers, after all.

If an appointment is made by a doctor's office or healthcare institution, the patient should be seen in a time frame that isn't counted in hours but minutes and preferably seconds. Who knows, we might start a new trend here.

If you don't respond to customers promptly, you are asking for all kinds of problems. People are busy, and we don't like to wait. There are other businesses waiting to take away that business.

I know everyone is trying harder and many healthcare executives and physicians are very aware of the problems that can occur when patients are kept waiting too long. But no matter what business you are in, if you don't recognize the trend for getting things quickly you are heading for trouble.

Sure, it's a shame we are all so busy and so stressed. But that's the reality of modern-day living. We are all trying to squeeze more and more into our lives on a daily basis, and when we don't get served quickly we react negatively. So faster and more efficient is the name of the game, and you had better be prepared to get on the field of play. Be quick about it.

Take time to listen
In sales, it's as important as talking

I've written extensively about listening and how essential it is for effective communication. I think that's reflected in the number of books published and seminars conducted on the value of listening in both the professional sense and on the personal level. But because of some recent experiences I thought it might be worth repeating. Why my continuing concern? It has to do with some people I interviewed recently for sales openings at *Modern Healthcare* and *Modern Physician*. Many of these individuals are highly experienced, so you would assume that by now they would know when to talk and when to listen. But to my surprise, the seasoned pros often made the same mistake as those with less experience—they spoke before they understood the ground rules. Some of the people I interviewed were so excited to talk about their accomplishments and work history that they forgot to let me speak first and outline what I'm looking for in a salesperson. Enthusiasm is welcome. In fact I expect it, because nobody can be successful in sales without it. But sales pros—all professionals, for that matter—can't afford to forget the basics. And listening is one of them.

I've always taught young salespeople to simply introduce themselves to a potential client at the start of their calls and then sit back and let the customers do the talking. They'll provide the verbal clues about what they want from you. If you're smart you'll listen intently. Then start your sales pitch by matching your selling points to the needs the client describes to you. But too often salespeople will be so nervous and wired that they forget to listen first and ask questions later. They go into their pitch without understanding what the client wants. Patience is truly a virtue here. It sounds so basic, but every day salespeople come out of calls wondering why they have lost the sales "touch." The only thing they've really lost is a respect for the fundamentals.

Several years ago one of the top salespeople at *Modern Healthcare* came to me in tears. She was having a bad year and couldn't understand why. She was frustrated and depressed by what was happening. I asked her all sorts of questions, but we couldn't figure out what the problem was. I then suggested we make a trip together. I had always enjoyed being with her because she loved selling and it was fun to watch her perform. During the first call we made together, her problem became evident. Before she even sat down in the chair she started to talk over her client who was telling her, "Hey, don't sell me, I've just sent in an order for 12 pages." His comments didn't even register with her. She was just too intense. I had to say: "Stop! He just gave you the order." She was stunned. She looked at me with a puzzled look, and then she realized what she had done.

However, during the very next call, it happened again.

Later that evening we talked at length about what I had witnessed during her calls. She was delighted that I had come along with her and was able to discover what was going on. Sometimes we're not even aware that we have a problem. Listening is one of the most effective tools available to become a better salesperson, but it takes discipline. A lot of peddlers don't have that willingness to be disciplined. They think they know all the moves, but in reality they're doomed to failure. Our customers are no different from you and me. They want to be heard, and we should give them every opportunity to speak first. It's a matter of good manners and smart selling.

I always find it amazing how effective real listening can be and how it applies to every aspect of life. See for yourself. Make an extra effort to truly listen, whether it's with your spouse, your children or your best friend. It's a special way to show others how much you care about them and their needs. You'll be surprised by what you hear and what you learn. It works.

Chapter 3

LEADERSHIP

THE BASIC RECIPE FOR A LEADER

Start with a positive outlook, and add savvy, charisma,
humility and humor

I talk a lot about leadership, and when I do, I speak from experience, having interacted with innumerable leaders in the business world, the military and sports. One thing I know for sure is that being a leader isn't easy: It takes patience, persistence and age, as well as the ability to deal with ambiguity.

Every employee is different, with a different background and work experience, so what inspires one person might not necessarily motivate another. Leadership is a complicated thing involving multiple skills, some of them learned, many of them innate. That's why not everyone is cut out to be a leader.

There's no doubt about it, no matter how many courses you take or books you read on the subject, walking the walk of leadership is a complicated and tricky business. It can either be the most rewarding experience a person has or it can be the most debilitating, both mentally and physically.

It all starts with attitude. I have always declared that attitude is everything, but too many people just don't get it. People with a positive outlook on life can accomplish just about anything. They don't let doom-and-gloomers take their dreams away; they devise a plan and then persuade others to join them in accomplishing their goals.

But there are other ingredients that any leader should have to succeed. One is street smarts, which come from experience. Leaders who don't have experience usually end up befuddled when faced with stressful, chaotic situations. They simply don't know what to do and freeze up. A similar skill is plain common sense, and you don't learn that in books. It comes from experience.

The art of leadership is somewhat fragile, and there are intangibles some individuals have that others do not. It's hard to define charisma, the natural ability to charm others and get them to follow you, but the fact is, some people seem to be born to lead. Another word is class, the people who through integrity, passion and intellect naturally rise to the top. Classy people always conduct themselves in an appropriate way with ease and maturity, and others are attracted to them. You know these people when you see them.

There is a great deal of difference between a leader who does things naturally and one who has learned how to lead. Both, by the way, can be effective, but the ability to inspire and motivate usually comes more easily to one whose life experiences have given that person street smarts or common sense. It's hard to be any more definitive on this point. Charisma can't be taught, although you can be taught leadership skills. The military has had a phenomenal record of teaching leadership. The armed forces have a terrific track record of molding leaders for both combat and peacetime.

I have seen individuals who on paper look like they have all the ingredients to be effective leaders but who never quite rise to the occasion. Something is missing. They have the right diplomas and they look the part, but they cannot articulate a vision, which can be a disaster. Most effective leaders in any field are able to describe to their colleagues what it is they hope to accomplish and how a job can be done. Before you have teamwork, you have to have a goal, and that's where the leader comes in.

On the other hand, one of the other essential leadership traits is the ability and willingness to listen. Quality leaders always have the innate ability to listen with their eyes, ears and instincts. They need to watch how their subordinates behave, how they react when they are instructed to do something or when things don't go their way. Then there is listening to someone who comes to you for no other reason than that he or she respects you. When a colleague comes up with a new idea or is even critical about the way things are going, a leader must listen.

Then there is a far more elusive trait that every quality leader should have, and that is humility. I am consistently blown away by those individuals in leadership positions who believe a company or organization revolves around them. They seem to have bouts of amnesia about their colleagues who do the heavy lifting and make the boss look good. Leaders who take all the credit are not the kind who can take an organization to the next level of excellence. In fact, when you look at companies in Chapter 11, you often find arrogant leadership behind the failure. Arrogance translates into insensitivity, which leads to bad decision making. Top-flight leaders know that without the support and sacrifices of their colleagues they won't be successful, so they cultivate their relationships and make a point of recognizing others' work.

Another element of humility is being able to joke, especially about your own foibles. Most healthcare CEOs I know have a well-developed sense of humor. There's nothing like a good laugh to relieve stress and survive the pressures a leader must confront every day. Even if you aren't making a joke, the old adage, "smile, and the world smiles with you," is so true. People love to be with others who have a smile on their face and enjoy life. Nobody wants to be with people who see the glass half empty. Just for fun walk down a hall or into a room with a big smile on your face. It makes all the difference in the world.

Leadership is complex, it's much more than what I have outlined here. There are all kinds of books on how to lead others, but too often the academics forget some of the basics. They put forth ethereal philosophies that seem to be derived from some ancient Eastern culture. Many things have changed that have made some of these leadership ideas outdated.

But there are some values that will never change and must be adhered to for success. These are the skills of being able to make others follow you toward clearly defined goals and treating everyone with dignity and respect. Don't try to reinvent the wheel on leadership, just stick with the basics. Start with a smile.

Make your workers the stars
Good leadership means cultivating, motivating your family of employees

I recently had breakfast with Terry Mulligan, an old friend who has had a distinguished career in healthcare manufacturing, having been the top sales honcho at American Hospital Supply Co. when the great Karl Bays ran the show. After Baxter International bought American Hospital, Terry, who is now retired, became the top sales executive at the combined firm under another great leader, Vernon Loucks Jr. Terry and I always enjoy swapping sales stories, and many times our discussions turn to leadership.

On this occasion Terry told me a story about being an army lieutenant stationed in Germany in the 1960's. One night he was given the duty of running the motor pool. That night a deep fog came up, making any driving treacherous. The motor pool's first sergeant suggested that Lt. Mulligan close down the pool and Terry agreed. The next day a full colonel came to visit Terry, and asked him why he had closed the motor pool the previous night. "Because, sir, the first sergeant asked me to," Terry recalled. No sooner had the words left his mouth than the colonel lectured him on what it meant to be a commander. As an officer, Terry should have been the one to make the decision, not the first sergeant, the colonel said.

What the colonel was really saying was that leaders have to lead and be the ones to make the key decisions, said Terry, who serves on a number of healthcare company boards.

Terry has a lot of sayings, and here are a couple that are relevant to this topic. The first is, "Good people beget good people and bad people beget bad people." What he means is that leaders reinforce personality traits in the people they lead, for good or for ill. Leaders can make everyone around them better through example and wisdom or they can cultivate negativity and poor performance through their actions or inaction.

That leads to another Mulliganism, which is, "People want to be led, not managed." People want someone to mentor and inspire them, not micromanage their every action and second-guess them when they do their jobs.

I get lots of letters from readers and I appreciate all of them, even the ones that aren't good news. These letters help me understand what's going on in readers' minds and motivate me in my job as publisher of a magazine, and that in turn motivates readers to do better in theirs. The letters that distress me the most are the ones that tell me about all the inane workplace policies and regulations that rob perfectly loyal and hardworking employees of their dignity and their standing within the company.

These letters aren't from spoiled employees who think the world owes them a living. These are from experienced professionals who know the score and simply are fed up with bosses who don't trust them to do their jobs and who don't respect them for who they are.

A healthcare institution should be like a family where everyone is treated with dignity and understanding and is recognized for their successes. Unfortunately, I often hear things such as this comment a healthcare executive made to me in a recent letter: "We are surrounded by fear-filled leadership."

I hear the same theme over and over. Managers worrying more about their careers than those of the people who report to them, taking credit for any good thing that happens in their department or institution and blaming problems on everyone but themselves. That isn't leadership by any definition.

Of course, healthcare isn't the only industry in which this is happening. We have witnessed a paucity of leadership in corporate America almost across the board. But healthcare ought to be different. This is a profession that is all about caring. It is more a calling than an occupation. And yes, it is a challenge, especially today. A healthcare leader has to be a magician. He or she is expected to be popular with the physicians, the board and the community. There is huge pressure on healthcare institutions faced with new regulatory burdens, rising costs and staffing shortages.

But that doesn't mean leaders can simply dump their problems on their staff or treat them as if they are cogs in a wheel. Any institution is only as good as the people who work there. If those people feel mistrusted, if they are sent memos worded like military manuals, if they aren't seen as individuals, then that institution will suffer. And the chief will suffer right along with it.

Leaders can attend all the management seminars they want or read all the books on the topic, but if they don't have a feel for their employees, they eventually will fail.

My advice for all managers is simple. Be with your people. Mentor them. Explain in person any new policies and why they are being implemented. Consult with staff. Ask them for advice. Don't hide behind memos. Get into the trenches with people to understand what workers are faced with. All of this takes an enormous amount of time, but it's the only way to lead. Call it being a member of the family.

Making your workers the stars of the show not only will improve morale but productivity as well. Managers have to be aware that their employees watch everything their bosses do. They need inspiration and they need your motivation—especially when they hear how tough things are in their industry. They need perspective and they need pride. Give them those things and then watch how incredibly creative your people can be. They belong to you, leader, and they are what you are all about. You don't have to take a course to figure that out. Give of yourself and reap the rewards.

LEADING THE WAY
Managers are important, but leaders really make things happen

I recently had lunch with a top healthcare association executive. During the meal we got on the topic of the difference between leaders and managers. His contention was that too many people confuse the two. He feels that leaders are born, not made, and went on to say that leaders "come out of the cradle that way." I'm not sure I agree with his thesis, but it sure makes for an interesting discussion. It seems my friend had attended a leadership meeting and his observation was, "They seemed to be talking more about managing than actual leadership." Over the past few days I've thought a great deal about leadership vs. managing, and the more I think about it the more I believe my friend may have a point.

One of the main characteristics of a great leader is courage. The courage to believe in one's own vision and destiny, the courage to actually lead, the courage to give colleagues authority and power, as well as the courage to behave like a fool occasionally.

A manager, on the other hand, might oversee a certain department or region so that it performs efficiently and productively. Managers have to sort through all kinds of challenges, including bureaucracies, to make sure things get done. Like leaders, it takes a great deal of intestinal fortitude to run anything these days. While speaking to the dean of a prestigious business school, I was told that more and more of his brightest students make it clear that they want nothing to do with being managers.

During the discussion with my friend, memories of my basic training days in the U.S. Army during the Korean War came flooding back. There was a certain corporal I've always remembered. To this day, I can see Cpl. Burleson calling all of the private E-2s outside at 5 a.m. to get into formation. In those days, basic training consisted of eight weeks of infantry training and an additional eight weeks of training related to whatever specialty you had been assigned.

I was assigned to the medical corps and most of us in that group were college graduates and therefore thought we were light years ahead of our noncommissioned instructors. At least, that's the way a lot of us felt at the beginning of our grinding infantry regimen. How arrogant and stupid we were to feel that way. Burleson was gangly, about 6 feet 5 inches tall and spoke with a heavy Southern drawl. He only had an eighth-grade education and though he had seen live action in Korea, he never said a word about it. Burleson wasn't a "yeller" like the typical platoon leader. I never saw him embarrass a soldier in front of the ranks and I never heard him use profanity, although I'm sure he knew all the words. Burleson trained us like his life depended on it because he knew our lives depended on it. He understood that a lot of us would see action and that some of us might not return home.

When basic training ended, every one of us took the time to tell the corporal how much he meant to us. That's when I realized college degrees or above-average intelligence doesn't have a lot to do with leadership. Through his demeanor, example and respectful treatment of others, Burleson showed his men why we should believe in him.

There is something magical about leaders. If you are lucky enough to be in their presence, they often give off a sense of confidence, enthusiasm and magic that is hard to define, even though many books have been written on the subject.

To me a great leader simply has "it." He or she is able to inspire and motivate people through passion, a sense of mission and vision. Leaders' enthusiasm and dedication are contagious and when they undertake something, others follow.

Managers, on the other hand, usually are pretty good technicians who know the importance of crossing the t's and dotting the i's; the good ones are goal-oriented, focused and make sure their group is headed in the right direction. Although they have courage, focus and responsibility, they are not always inclined to take risks. A leader, on the other hand, has no problem with risks and takes them. Successful business was started by an individual who knew risk was essential to success. And those kinds of leaders are why American businesses are the envy of the rest of the world.

I have met a number of entrepreneurs in my life and always have been impressed that they are so focused on the success of their ideas that they don't pay attention to details. Entrepreneurs make it happen and often embody leadership characteristics. That isn't to say they are bad businesspeople, it's just that they are so focused on getting their businesses up and running that they often don't spend the time necessary to make sure things are in order. That's why so many of them bring financial advisers in to help them in the early stages of their venture or eventually recruit managers.

The point is this: There is a distinct difference between a leader and a manager. A manager supervises, while a leader makes things happen. But the really smart leader recognizes his shortcomings and makes sure he brings to his executive team the very best managers he can find to ensure things run properly. He also makes sure he gets out of their way so they can do their jobs.

One of the great tragedies of business today is that too many managers are in positions that require the special talent of leadership. They have been given those jobs because too many boards and other high-level executives still don't recognize the difference between leaders and managers. Often, when a manager is put into a position of leadership he or she spends so much time micromanaging others that they stifle creativity and spontaneity. Without those two things, businesses usually fail. Look around you. The evidence is all over the place.

INSPIRING OTHERS

Good leaders are encouraging and supportive

If you can motivate others, you have a talent others would give their eye teeth to possess. We're all looking to free the genie who will give us the ability to help others excel. It's a continuing challenge for leaders in all disciplines. Look around you and watch managers trying to get the most out of their people. Some do it with aplomb while others fall flat on their faces. Some people have that certain ability to get others to go the extra mile. Others, in their attempts to motivate, only turn people off. If you think you're in the latter category, I suggest you get a copy of *Unleash the Potential—Unlocking the Mystery of Motivation* by David Zimmerman. The author has been around healthcare for 30 years and for many years was chairman and chief executive officer of his own consulting firm in Milwaukee. The firm is now headed by his son, Michael. He has also written 10 other books on a host of diverse subjects relating to healthcare. His latest work hits home for all of us trying to do more with less.

We all like to be inspired. It's simply human nature. The absence of inspiration can lead to boredom, dissatisfaction and poor morale. Many companies experience this problem and don't know why. Zimmerman explains it this way: "It is human nature to be dissatisfied with the status quo. Dissatisfaction gives rise to desire. Satisfaction is actually the absence of motivation." As Lawrence Miller has observed in *American Spirit*, "I have never met an excellent executive who was satisfied." Author Dean Spitzer has said: "I would go even further: I have never met an excellent human being who was satisfied. People may become accustomed to mediocrity, but they are never motivated by it."

People want to reach higher levels of performance. It's our nature, but without motivation something in us withers and dies. Often it's the way we are led. For instance, Zimmerman points out that in a survey from *Young Executive Magazine*, these 10 annoying habits of managers were highlighted: "Is a poor communicator; lies; is indecisive; favors 'suck-ups'; does not listen;

procrastinates; is forgetful; withholds information; belittles employees publicly; talks too much." Obviously, anyone who embodies even some of those habits is going to come up short in motivational ability.

Zimmerman then quotes a fellow consultant, Dennis Moore, who shared his personal experiences in dealing with hospital executives and their inability to motivate others. Moore cites three attitudes that seem to get in the way. He describes one such attitude this way: "I'm more knowledgeable about what should happen in this area than anyone else; that's why I was made the manager!" Another blocking attitude is this one: "It took me a long time to get to this point where I have the authority to do things my way, the right way, and I'm not about to give up that power." And I bet we've all run into this one: "If I let others do the job, no matter how well I explain it, for some reason they never do it just like I would. This ineptitude forces me to do more things than I would like, but in order to get them done right I have no other choice." Leaders who exhibit any of these self-defeating attitudes just won't cut it when it comes to motivating others.

Zimmerman is very clear about what he sees as essential traits for effective motivators. They include being humble, being a good listener and celebrating the triumphs of colleagues. The key here is making others feel important. There should be no greater reward for leaders than to see others grow and advance, knowing that without their encouragement and mentoring, their colleagues might not have attained such success. Zimmerman also shares another valuable insight: If we hope to have the ability to motivate others, we must be motivated by being passionate about everything we do. Zimmerman offers a blueprint for any leader who's willing to learn. Inspire others.

QUALITY LEADERS LEARN FROM THEIR MISTAKES
And they're big enough to admit when they are wrong

There are plenty of books on management and leadership. I read as many as I can but too often find some to be lacking in meaningful insight and practicality That definitely isn't the case, however, with *The Leadership Engine—How Winning Companies Build Leaders at Every Level* (HarperBusiness) by Noel M. Tichy with Eli Cohen. Tichy, also co-author of *Control Your Destiny or Someone Else Will,* is a professor at the University of Michigan Business School specializing in leadership and organizational transformation. He's been a consultant to General Electric since 1982 and for two years ran GE's Crotonville executive development center. As a senior partner in Action Learning Associates he has consulted with some of the top corporations worldwide such as Royal Dutch/Shell, Coca-Cola, Mercedes-Benz, Ameritech, NEC and Royal Bank of Canada. Not since I first read Max DePrees's *Leadership is an Art* have I been so energized by a book on leadership.

As a matter of fact, in one "Publisher's Letter" I talked about many of the points Tichy covers but failed to mention his book about talented leaders and highly effective organizations. To make his case, Tichy not only includes vignettes about well-known executives in corporate America but also discusses inspirational leaders like Phil Jackson, former head coach of the Chicago Bulls and now head coach of the Los Angeles Lakers, and military leaders like General Wayne Downing, former head of U.S. Special Forces, and Rear Admiral Ray Smith, a former Navy SEAL. Tichy holds the highest regard for those leaders who are willing to develop a culture of mentoring at all levels. It's a point he drove home at a luncheon presentation at the Economic Club of Chicago he shared with Bill Pollard, chairman of ServiceMaster. The audience of some 400 top movers and shakers was mesmerized by their messages.

For instance, Tichy says quality leaders draw from their pasts, explaining how events early in life became lessons they've used time and again. They consciously capture these lessons and use them as guides. At the Economic Club presentation, Tichy showed a dramatic video clip of Bob Knowling, a former vice president of Ameritech who now runs U S West's telephone network, talking about an incident when he was seven years old that served as the basis for his determination of values and ideals. The story is retold in Tichy's book: "Knowling, an African-American, was one of 13 children. He had gone to the welfare office with his mother to get food stamps. When she asked if she could use the stamps to buy more peanut butter and less of something else, the woman behind the counter told her: 'You wouldn't be here asking for more peanut butter if you had thought twice about having all those kids.' At that moment, Knowling says: 'I witnessed the transformation of my mother, and my own began as well.' She took my hand, and as we walked out of the office, she declared, 'I am off welfare for good.'" As Knowling's mother strived to make good on her promise, she also taught her children they must forever take responsibility for their own lives.

In a chapter titled "Edge—The Courage to See Reality and Act on It, " I read something, under the subheading "Truth and Courage" that I strongly believe in. I'll quote: "One way to tell if a leader has edge is if he or she is willing to publicly admit his or her mistakes. It's easy to overlook this telltale sign because it usually doesn't cause pain for anyone except the leader. But for the leader, it's the ultimate test of reality, the reality he or she was wrong. It is also a positive sign that the leader will accept the honest mistakes of others as well." In an age when so many people are quick to blame others for their own mistakes, one of the things that will never go out of style is when a leader shows character and candor by admitting he or she is just like everyone else—human. Truth is power.

NEEDED: BETTER COMMUNICATION
Management should keep <u>everyone</u> informed

Too frequently I hear the lament: "They don't communicate with us. We don't know what's going on half the time. I guess we just aren't important in the grand scheme of things." The people doing the talking are employees referring to the executives who run their companies. The managers apparently do a good job of communicating with one another, but they don't get the message to the people who really do the work and make their companies run smoothly. It's almost like the military, where the corporals and the sergeants are the ones who really run things. Sure, the officers give the orders, but without the noncoms any military unit would come to a grinding halt. It's the grunts who do the dirty work. The same goes for corporate life, but we overlook the obvious and forget that communicating with colleagues and peers is the sign of enlightened leadership.

The truth must also be part of the communication process. The employer of a good friend of mine recently went through a merger. Although my friend had been with her company for more than 20 years, she was excited about the merger's possibilities and championed the deal. She quoted the president of her company, who told employees that no radical changes would be forthcoming. Their jobs were safe, but maybe in a year or two there could be some minor adjustments. Unfortunately, she, along with a number of her colleagues, was given her walking papers a few days later. She's crushed, but with her talent she should land another job quickly. Such actions by executives are guaranteed to demoralize a work force.

Then on a recent speaking engagement I was met at the airport by a young woman who was to drive me to my destination. She was full of enthusiasm—and told me about all the exciting things that were going on within the healthcare system she worked for. Some of the developments were controversial because the system's goal was to bring together people from various organizations whose cultures were quite different. My question was whether her bosses were keeping her informed during the process. She didn't answer me right away but finally admitted they weren't. This person was committed and loyal, but management wasn't keeping her up-to-date on what was transpiring. Even though she wasn't a senior member in the organization, that shouldn't matter. Staffers at all levels deserve to know what's going on. When workers are left in the dark, morale eventually suffers and productivity falls. When that happens, her bosses will probably be mystified, but they will have only themselves to blame.

All kinds of strange things happen when people don't communicate. For instance, I recently heard the chief executive of a major hospital in a large metropolitan area recount the story of an unsuccessful merger with another hospital. Executives from both hospitals were on board. The physicians for the most part liked the idea, and both boards were in agreement. But the deal fell apart after only a few months. Why? Because the department heads, nurses and some physicians torpedoed the idea. They were left out of the loop, so they had no details about the plan. If somebody had simply been bright enough to involve these key workers from the beginning, odds are everything would have proceeded smoothly. People don't like to be ignored and taken for granted. Again, the key word is communication.

Without the right people, no organization can prosper. That will never change. But too often the very people who made an organization successful are forgotten as the focus shifts to the bottom line. What's wrong with us? Successful companies make sure they coddle their most precious assets—their workers. Be open and truthful.

Good leaders show respect
And they need to have the common touch

I've known Larry Mathis for years. He's had a long career and has held myriad leadership positions in healthcare. He chose to retire from a high profile job in 1997 as chief executive officer of Methodist Health Care System in Houston and join his wife, Diane Peterson, in her consulting business. Mathis has led both the American College of Healthcare Executives and the American Hospital Association, and there's no doubt he knows his stuff. He sent me a copy of his book, *The Mathis Maxims: Lessons in Leadership.* What I like best about the book is Mathis' honesty about the state of leadership right now and what he says any leader must aspire to if he or she wants to excel. While getting organized in a new office here in Chicago, I came across Mathis' book and took some time to reread certain chapters. I was even more impressed than I was a few months ago.

One section details Mathis' opinions about leadership qualities. Too many executives like to blame those who report to them for their own failures as leaders. They don't want to take the heat. That's arrogance, and it's a tactic of cowards. Such individuals have no place in leadership positions. Mathis also talks about how every individual has a valuable role in a given organization, but too often many of these people are not treated with dignity and respect. Great leaders instinctively understand the importance of the team; they don't discriminate between part-timers and senior executives. Everyone must contribute, but each person also needs to receive recognition for the effort. "I tried to treat everyone—surgeon, laundress, board member, gardener, nurse the same: with fairness, openness and respect," Mathis writes of his years as a top executive. "I have known executives who are superb at relating to their organizational superiors, but denigrate their subordinates. They schmooze their bosses; they scream at their secretaries ... You can't effectively lead others if you do not respect the dignity and worth of every person in the organization. Respect is the very foundation of leadership."

Another favorite section in the book is subtitled "The troops eat first." It's an old military dictum that officers take care of their troops' needs first. Only then do they address their own needs. That's hard for many leaders to grasp because of their backgrounds. People who have been on the front lines and fought through hard times have a pretty good idea of how to lead people who report to them. They can identify with their needs. But if people have never toiled in the trenches and have been shielded from life's challenges and injustices, they might not have an appreciation for what a quality leader needs to know.

Mathis understands another important point: "You don't get anywhere working for yourself—you must work for something bigger than yourself." Naturally, we all have personal dreams and set individual goals. But working solely for one's own needs and wants doesn't get the job done. This is where leaders must step in and make sure their employees have a goal to strive for—together. Look at the people in healthcare. Most caregivers are in this business because they believe helping others is a noble vocation. It's not just a job. But too many leaders do not know how to convey a sense of mission. When I meet with healthcare executives, I talk about what a great industry this is because it's all about improving quality of life. It's a movement for good that is unlike many other industries. It's day-to-day work that is almost guaranteed to involve life-and-death decisions. We're all lucky to be a part of it.

Rereading some of Mathis' book made me realize how important it is for leaders to have the common touch with every person they meet. Most leaders in healthcare get it, but many don't. For those who want to work on their leadership quotient—no matter what the industry—Mathis' book is a good place to start. We all need to brush up now and then.

Mathis has learned that if one wants to be a leader and has the energy and drive to do so, there will always be plenty of opportunity. But there is a price. Sometimes holding a leadership role can strain relationships or damage one's health.

Mathis has lots of other excellent pieces of advice. A few of my favorites:

- "Credit is rarely given, often taken."
- "After integrity, perseverance is an executive's most valuable trait."
- "You can teach an old dog new tricks. But you really shouldn't."
- "Be nice to everyone on the way up. You will need them on the way down."

Maximize your leadership skills...

FOLLOW YOUR INSTINCTS
A basic rule of management is knowing when a decision
doesn't feel quite right

Recently I had total left hip replacement surgery and consequently I've had some time to read and cogitate. I went through the same experience in March 2002 with my right hip. Even though I had what they term minimally invasive surgery, there was still plenty of invasion and a period of rehabilitation.

Staying at home is not my cup of tea. The one saving grace is that I get to spend a lot of time with my Alaskan malamute, Yodie. I also get to read things such as *The Wall Street Journal*, *The New York Times* and my hometown Chicago newspapers.

In a recent issue of the *Chicago Tribune*, an article caught my attention because it delivered a message that is absolutely essential for anyone in healthcare management.

What the story highlighted was how any of us should have confidence in our abilities and intuition. Too often we fail to trust our own instincts when it comes to making decisions that affect our businesses. Those decisions can be anything from hiring quality people, to how to approach a colleague about a new project, to whether to go with a new product development plan. It could be just about anything that has to do with the business of making decisions and the complications that can suddenly crop up while trying to get things in order.

The story I read was about a young woman who started her own women's fashion and bridal boutique after she graduated from a New York fashion design school in October 1992. Like any new small business, the first few months were tough, and if it hadn't been for family and friends coming in to buy things from her, she might have failed.

This young business owner got lucky when a buyer from a major department store chain happened into the shop. The buyer was impressed with the dresses and asked for more information and some samples for her boss, who was the head dress buyer at the store. Before the young entrepreneur knew it, she was supplying to three of the chain's stores. The future looked bright indeed, or so it seemed.

The shop owner tells her story this way: "My first delivery to the department store was a giant success. Then came the second delivery. The fabric had been ordered with plenty of lead time, but two weeks after it was due I got a call that there was a problem with the two stretch velvet colors I had ordered. The red velvet was on the way, but the black velvet was suddenly out of stock. 'Not to worry,' the fabric supplier said, 'there is a charming forest green to replace it.' I did not want to lose this order and there was no time to find a new supplier for the black stretch velvet. I was afraid if I shipped only the red color I would lose the whole order. I sent a fabric swatch to the buyer and much to my surprise it was approved."

Now this is where knowledge and instinct come into play. Our shop owner had second thoughts about her decision. "I knew better than to substitute green for black. After all, black makes you look slimmer, hides dirt and goes with everything. Women know this. Charming forest green does none of these things, but I figured the buyer, with all her years of experience and multimillion-dollar stores, knew more than I did."

Actually our young shop owner had a better fix on trends than the buyer because in the end none of the stretch green velvet dresses sold. As a matter of fact, the entrepreneur had to give the department store what is termed "markdown money." Apparently, in the dress design business this is a fairly common standard practice of credit given to the store by the designer to cover the store's profit margin when merchandise has to be marked down. For the designer it was a major blow and almost caused financial disaster. But she survived the ordeal and is still doing well with her business.

What she learned from the experience was this: "My mistake was not trusting my gut. I literally get a sick feeling in my stomach when something doesn't feel right. These days I do what my gut tells me to do, The feeling in the pit of my stomach is something I have learned not to ignore. My biggest mistake was a very costly and very embarrassing mistake."

At a young age this young entrepreneur learned to trust her own judgment. I've read many management books where this thesis is set forth. I've also talked to many managers and executives who have told me some of their biggest mistakes happened because they didn't follow their own "inner voice."

Sure it's tough to trust your own instincts in complicated circumstances, but most of us have had enough experience in our chosen profession to know when something doesn't feel quite right. I've had it happen to me and I'm sure you have, too.

Having confidence in one's own instincts is vitally important to any manager or leader. Experience and knowledge, of course, play into it, but that intangible "instinct" can be more important than anything else in the total equation.

The story of the dress designer is a simple way to illustrate this point. She learned very early in her career to trust herself, and that's what a lot of us need to remember in our own business dealings. No matter what the data or evidence of a particular matter purports to show, your instincts can be invaluable in assessing a matter. Trust yourself.

THE OTHER SIDE OF MENTORING
Those receiving wisdom must keep their ears and minds open

At the beginning of your career there are always those experiences that leave a lasting impression, much like some early lessons we learned in childhood.

Young people are both vulnerable and innocent in terms of what is expected of them and what they have to do to be productive and successful. It is a critical time in anyone's career, and if you are not lucky enough to have a good boss who has solid values and a willingness to guide you on the right course, those first few weeks can leave you disillusioned and cynical. But sometimes people outside your organization offer advice and guidance that can be invaluable.

I know when I started in publishing I had bosses who showed me the ropes, but there were clients who helped me just as much by giving me advice about a presentation I had made or how I should proceed in selling accounts.

People can be very giving when it comes to advice, but those who are receiving the mentoring have to be willing to listen and keep an open mind. Many people begin their careers by thinking they know more than anybody else—including their managers—about how to do their jobs. That's the road to failure. An open mind is the opposite—the key to future success.

This whole topic came to mind because of a story I was told recently by a good friend who is one of the top salespeople for his company. The organization is one of the biggest operations in the industry and enjoys a wonderful reputation both in and out of healthcare. Over lunch this gentleman and I started trading sales stories and talking about how important it is to get off on the right foot in life. I told him how lucky I have been in my sales career to have great bosses who guided me through some rough times. I was especially fortunate to have great mentors at the very beginning of my career and I will always remember how patient they were with me.

My friend then told me a story about making his first call as a detail salesman for a major drug manufacturer. Here's what he told me:

"I went through all the training the company gave their sales reps. It was all very comprehensive, and after completing it I couldn't wait to make my first call. I remember telling my wife how excited I was and I also told her I was nervous, but out the door I went to make my first call. My first appointment was with a general practitioner. I was really geared up to give him the works. But as I was beginning my pitch he stopped me cold. I was stunned and I started to speak again, but he held up his hand and asked me for the card that detailed the contraindications and side effects. Then he asked me to tell him what were the side effects and contraindications for the new drug. I was stumped and embarrassed. I didn't know the answer to his question and he told me to come back another time and detail him on another drug that my company sold.

"I well remember going home right after that call and telling my wife I didn't think I was cut out for the drug business. She told me I was wrong because she felt what the physician had done was both positive and instructive. A couple of weeks later, I called on that doctor again and gave him a presentation on another drug. This time I knew all the side effects and contraindications, and he gave me an order. That lesson he taught me was so important because from that day forward I knew everything I needed to know when I made calls on physicians. The lesson I learned was always to be prepared and always to know the product or products you are presenting. That physician and I are still good friends and I honestly believe he helped make my career a success."

Another wonderful story I heard recently on this subject comes from my good friend Jan Jennings, former chief executive officer of Jefferson Regional Medical Center in Pittsburgh and now with American Healthcare Solutions. Like so many of his peers, he loves the healthcare industry and over the years has distinguished himself as one of the most dynamic and capable leaders in the industry. Here's what he said in an e-mail.

"Twenty-five years ago, I was serving on the administrative staff of Shadyside Hospital. The CEO asked me to serve on a committee of the Hospital Council of Western Pennsylvania. The chairwoman of the HCWP committee was Sister Ferdinand Clark, then the president and CEO of Mercy Hospital of Pittsburgh. She was quite a woman. She was respected and admired by all who knew her. In one of those HCWP committee meetings we were discussing something of no particular importance and one of the men on the committee uttered an old expression on reference to the matter at hand. He said to Sister Ferdinand, 'Don't worry about it. The devil is in the details.' Her response changed my career. She said, 'Young man, no, that is not right The devil is not in the details—God lives in the details. You must look into the details in order to find the truth.' "

I couldn't possibly do credit to Jennings' commentary, but after briefly outlining his career he tells the story of his best friend's adult son, who had a terrible trauma to his left arm. He was rushed to a trauma center where surgery was performed. Later he would have additional surgery at St. Clair Memorial Hospital, also in Pittsburgh. Jennings' friend expected a good experience from the surgery because St. Clair has an excellent reputation. What he didn't expect was a flawless hospital experience.

In Jennings' words, "Suffice it to say, the contrast (with the first hospital) was dramatic. What St. Clair demonstrated with this episode was flawless attention to detail. The cleanliness, the crisp linens, the quality food and the hospitable, well-trained and highly motivated personnel are the product of meticulous planning and superb execution.

"To be more specific, you find the devil in some American hospitals when you observe dirty hospital rooms, poor outcomes, unwarranted nosocomial infections, lousy food, gruff personnel and poor communication with the patient and family. Thank God this example at St. Clair Hospital is rapidly becoming the norm of American hospital care. So Sister Ferdinand was right, God lives in the details."

Jennings has never forgotten Sister Ferdinand's words, and because of her philosophy his career has been filled with success.

ADVICE FOR A NEW GENERATION
What I would like to say to the high school graduates

A good friend recently asked if I could give him some ideas for a commencement address he was to give at the high school in his hometown. He is a very successful executive and has attained a reputation not only for his integrity and honesty but also his dedication to his company, his colleagues and his deep feelings about the healthcare industry.

I sent him some of my thoughts and also would like to share them with you, for they carry resonance even for those of us for whom high school was something we left behind a long time ago.

Here is what I would tell the graduates:

Congratulations on your major achievement. For each of you this day is the start of something different, as different as each of you are as individuals. Many of you will go on to college, others will join a branch of the military and still others will start your work lives.

Whatever you choose to do, you are about to embark on a journey filled with opportunity and promise. After all, in the United States of America you are free to be just about anything you want to be.

I remember being in your shoes with the conflicting emotions you probably are feeling. Your friends, the people you have shared your lives with, are heading off in different directions. There are the teachers who guided you who will be left behind.

Soon, you will leave your parents for the first time to be out on your own. After this ceremony, some of you will never see each other again. Take the time to say goodbye.

There is the excitement of new challenges. For those going on to college, a new set of friends, ideas and experiences awaits.

A good friend of mine once told me that the three most important priorities in life are love of family, love of friends and love of work. I can attest to you that those are the three things I treasure most. Notice that common word, love. It's so important in everything we do in life. The longer I am on this earth the more I realize how critically important it is to have love in your life, to love life itself and to feel passionate about what you are doing.

This attitude toward life can and must be cultivated if you are to succeed out there in the world. I always have treasured the words of theologian Charles Swindoll: "The longer I live, the more I realize the impact of attitude on life. Attitude, to me, is more important than facts. It is more important than the past, than education, than money, than circumstances, than failures, than successes, than what other people think or say or do. It is more important than appearance, giftedness or skill. It will make or break a company, a church, a home.

"The remarkable thing is we have a choice every day regarding the attitude we will embrace for that day. We cannot change our past ... we cannot change the inevitable. The only thing we can do is play on the one string we have, and that is our attitude. I am convinced that life is 10% what happens to me and 90% how I react to it. And so it is with you. We are in charge of our attitudes."

And so are you. One attitude to cultivate is to always respect the needs of others. Treating everyone with dignity and respect is essential for productive living, whether it be at work or anywhere else you deal with others. Good manners are a big part of respect. Say "please" and "thank you" when asking for assistance.

Be forthright and honest in everything you do. Don't follow the crowd on ethics. Your integrity is the most valuable thing you will have throughout your life and to lose that would be a disaster. Believe in yourself and what you stand for and don't be afraid to be principled in everything you do.

In fact, march to the beat of your own drummer for everything. Follow your own dreams and make your own decisions about what you do for a living, what organizations to join, what friends to make, what goals to pursue.

Don't be afraid of making mistakes. You learn far more from mistakes than from those situations where you happen to get something right the first time. We live in a society where everyone panics if they do something wrong, not realizing they have opened up the possibility of really gaining some insight into things.

Finally, let me leave you with some advice from someone who believes he has been the luckiest person in the world. As you begin a new adventure, judge your success by the degree you are enjoying peace, health and love.

Without any one of them life seems empty. Winning a sporting event, accumulating material things, coming out ahead on a business deal all make you feel good for a while, but that feeling never lasts. The things that count, that can't be bought, negotiated or won are peace, health and love. If you achieve them, you will be truly successful. The future is yours.

Chapter 4

SALESMANSHIP

TALKING ABOUT SALES
New book lays out the keys to the art of connecting with customers

As a salesperson for most of my life, I have always enjoyed books on the business of selling. I've read a number of them to learn how other sales professionals practice the art of persuading people to buy their products and services. Some of them are very worthwhile, although they tend to cover many of the same bases. One interesting thing about these how-to-sell books is that the same points they make about good salesmanship also apply to leadership. The basic ingredient for success in any field, of course, is the ability to communicate effectively, both in written and spoken word. Unless that skill is there, nobody gets very far in any top position. In leadership, communication is the key to translating vision into action. In sales, effective communication allows you to gain the confidence of a prospect or customer.

You can't communicate until you have something to talk about. For salespeople that entails knowing about the product you are selling, knowing about your prospect's business and understanding how the product or service you are selling will make the customer's operation more productive and efficient. One of the best books on selling I recently have read was authored by a gentleman who for nearly 10 years sold medical equipment to doctors, hospitals and HMOs before becoming vice president of purchasing for a national home-care company. Len Serafino's book is called *Sales Talk: How to Power Up Sales Through Verbal Mastery*. Serafino knows his stuff and has written an excellent primer for anyone in sales whether experienced or just starting out. It covers all the bases. One of the early chapters is titled "Read, Read, Read." He advises salespeople to not only read trade journals but also *Business Week, Fortune, Newsweek* and *The Wall Street Journal*. It doesn't mean the salesperson has to read every word, but it pays just to go through and peruse a periodical or magazine for new ideas that may be of interest to a client.

Serafino says sales presentations start with preparation.

Organize your information and put in the time and effort to winnow the presentation down to the essentials. Trying to wing it these days just doesn't work, but too many salespeople still try it with customers. Look, everybody's time is so precious these days that none of us has time to listen to someone who really doesn't know where they are headed with a sales pitch.

Passion, high energy and sincerity are essential to any good presentation and that takes practice, discipline and focus. Serafino quotes Roger Ailes, who pointed out in his book, *You Are The Message: Getting What You Want By Being Who You Are,* that research shows we begin to make up our minds about people within seven seconds of meeting them. That doesn't give any of us much time to gain someone's attention and trust.

The author goes on to discuss other points, but the main keys to me are listening, dress and writing.

I believe listening skills are the best tools available to anybody who wants to persuade others to do something. Too many people are so caught up in what they want to say they forget to listen with their eyes, ears and heart. Listening isn't only hearing the words someone speaks but actually absorbing what the other person has to say. There are unspoken clues people give while talking that let us know the full context of what they want to communicate, but you have to be really paying attention to get them. This isn't easy. It takes practice and concentration. You have to use not just your ears but also your eyes and mind.

There are times, for example, when it's best to end a call on a client abruptly when you see they either are preoccupied or just don't have the time to pay attention to what you have to say. Be aware of your customer's time and don't ever waste it.

The dress part should be a no-brainer but isn't. Serafino believes "business casual" is still OK, as long as everything is clean and pressed. However, I believe that era is drawing to a close, at least in sales. For my part, casual dress on any sales call is simply unprofessional. If you are going to plunk down tens of thousands of dollars on a product or service, you don't want to hand it over to someone who looks less than professional. In these leaner, more-competitive times, every little edge is important. People are impressed by people who take pride in how they present themselves, and Serafino makes this point very clear in his book.

Finally, there's writing. Knowing what to say and how to say it can be learned relatively easily, but it takes practice and organization. One of the most effective ways to get someone's attention is with a handwritten note. Think of it this way: What's the first thing you open when you get a bunch of letters at home? I bet it's those letters that have been addressed to you in ink. That also goes for the office. Take time to pen a note in ink and watch the magic. We all crave attention, and a handwritten letter really cuts through all the clutter at the office or home.

So for anyone in sales or just wanting to do a better job of communicating, try reading *Sales Talk*. It covers all the bases.

Listen to This

Take the time, make the effort to really hear what others need to tell you

As a frequent business traveler I am always meeting all kinds of people. I love that part of my job because most people are very nice, wherever I happen to be. I love people. I like to spend time with them and listen to their stories. I'm always amazed at how people open their hearts to perfect strangers on planes, in elevators and during other random encounters. We all need other people to tell things to, be they success stories, failures, worries or dreams. Sometimes we just need someone to be there in the early morning hours or when something traumatic occurs.

Loneliness can be a killer, yet many of us go through emotional crises thinking that no one else really understands what is happening to us. So it is important to hear others out when they come to you and ask for help or assistance. Sometimes all they really want is for you to sit and listen. Over the years I have learned to do just that, even when I have other things I have to do. When someone important to me wants to talk, I take the time to do so. I may have an important event coming up, but I have found I usually can take the time to listen if someone needs me to.

One of the best books I've read on this topic was sportswriter Mitch Albom's 1997 best seller, *Tuesdays with Morrie.* In the book, Albom's old college professor, Morrie Schwartz, talks about things that are so basic and yet profound. The jacket to the book gives a most adequate synopsis of its contents: "Maybe it was a grandparent, or a teacher, or a colleague. Someone older, patient and wise, who understood you when you were young and searching, helped you see the world as a more profound place, gave you sound advice to help you make your way through it. For Mitch Albom, that person was Morrie Schwartz, his college professor of nearly 20 years before. Maybe, like Mitch, you lost track of this mentor as you made your way, and the insights faded and the world seemed colder. Wouldn't you like to see that person again, ask the bigger questions that still haunt you, receive wisdom for your busy life today the way you once did when you were younger?" Albom's book is about the author's second chance to learn from his old mentor who was dying. Albom visits his old professor every Tuesday, which as it turns out was his habit when he was in college. Mostly, Albom listens and learns.

He learns about death, fear, aging, greed, marriage, family, society, forgiveness and what is a meaningful life. There isn't anything in there that wouldn't be interesting to any one of us. It has to do with our very essence as human beings and how we behave in the world, but for me it is mainly about those two things: listening and learning.

The book shows that if we pay attention, we can learn from everyone. The mentor also can learn from the student. In a recent conversation, an executive coach told me that one of the first things he has to do with the people he works with is to urge them to listen more intently to their colleagues. "The top executives feel time pressures all the time," the coach said. "They have very little time to themselves, and when they meet with their key people they have a tendency to ask a lot of questions, but because they are under the gun they don't really listen to what they are being told. A lot of bad decisions can be made as a result."

There are practical elements in the discipline of listening to others with one's mind and heart as well as ears. Top salespeople long ago realized that listening to customers about their needs and wants was much more important than trying to sell something to a client that they didn't need. Today, most enlightened companies will brag, "We listen to our customers." However, most retail businesses that I deal with seldom pay attention to the customers coming in their doors, and when they leave won't even make eye contact with them.

But the more sophisticated companies do, and they get most of their new ideas about products from their customers. That's the secret of success in today's selling environment. Customers want to be heard. Gone are the days of the fast-talking, back-slapping salesperson who does everything but listen. I submit to you that one of the reasons so many women have been successful in sales is because they were taught from an early age to listen to others.

MAKE THOSE FACE TO FACE CALLS
It's rule Number 1 in the world of sales

What's the most important thing any salesperson can do? From my perspective, it's making personal calls. Sure, doing business by phone is fine now and then. But the ultimate tool of any salesperson is the personal call. Today, however, we're told by consultants and experts that the sales business is changing. After all, this is the age of technology. These experts are telling corporate America that visiting customers and prospects is old-fashioned and inefficient. Of course, I've discovered that most of these "experts" don't have sales backgrounds. But that doesn't stop them. To them, making personal calls is cumbersome and too expensive. Don't listen to that kind of baloney.

Selling is a rough business. There's no easy way to do it. It takes much more than the latest piece of office technology. It takes people with courage and determination. Putting together a winning sales staff is tricky. Individuals who really love to sell and are willing to make the personal sacrifices necessary to succeed in the profession are hard to find. I don't care how impressive the resume looks or how many people interview a candidate, you really don't know how salespeople are going to work out until they are with you for a few months and are out spending time in an assigned territory.

So what's my beef? I think today's salespeople are misplacing their priorities. I hear more about problems with laptop computers than I do about how to get an appointment with a top prospect. I hear all kinds of discussions about "team play" in sales when most incentive programs are designed to reward individual efforts. Salespeople by instinct and training are mavericks and, in many cases, loners. I'm not saying they shouldn't use all the technological tools available to them or cooperate with other members of the organization. They do because they know it will help them do a better job. I'm just worried that maybe they're forgetting some principles of selling.

I think there's too much talk about the "new age" of selling without appreciating the fundamentals. A company can have the best product lines in the world, the most attractive brochures a marketing department can churn out and the most state-of-the-art laptops available; but if the sales force isn't communicating with clients and prospects, nothing is going to happen. It all begins with the personal call. That's what selling is all about. Everything else is incidental.

Salespeople should know their product lines cold. They also need to know their competitors' as well. Salespeople should spend more time out of the office than in, making as many personal calls as they can during a given day. They also should understand that selling isn't a 9-to-5 job. True sales pros work at their jobs seven days a week if that's what it takes. They also must understand that selling is done during the day, and paperwork and correspondence should be done during off hours.

Finally, remember there's nothing wrong with making money. It's the bottom line in the business world. If a company's salespeople are making a lot of money, they're obviously selling a lot of goods and services, and because of their hard work the company is probably making a nice profit as well. It sounds like a successful formula to me. Never be ashamed of that. Make an appointment.

IN PRAISE OF BREVITY
Sticking to the point is a lost art in the business world

I have discussed this before in this space, but recent encounters with some people have made it clear that it bears repeating: One of the most important tenets of common courtesy is to be considerate of other people's time. Sounds simple, doesn't it? If so, then I wonder why some people can't grasp it.

I find it almost unbelievable how inconsiderate some people are of the time constraints of colleagues and business contacts. They seem to think that the more they talk, the better their chances are of selling you something or bringing you around to their way of thinking. Actually, in most cases. the opposite is true. When a salesperson or a contact visits with me and goes on and on without sticking to the subject at hand, I get more and more irritated. A little small talk goes a long way.

Conversely, when someone comes into my office to sell me on an idea or talk about a matter and is organized and doesn't drone on, I am more receptive to what the person has to say. I realize this person has thought out what he or she wants to communicate to me and shows me the respect of sticking to the point and not wasting my valuable time. The word I'm trying to drive home is brevity.

Now I am not saying you shouldn't have relaxed conversations. In fact, there is nothing that beats the human touch. If you can't look into someone's eyes, how can you judge whether that person has integrity and is someone with whom you want to do business? Too often in our harried lives, however, we rely on electronic communications such as e-mail and voice mail. Of course, those have their purpose, but here's another way of looking at it: Think about how often a face-to-face meeting leaves you with a depth of feeling about that person and then ask yourself the last time you had that kind of reaction from an e-mail.

Even e-mail has its etiquette. In fact, e-mail is now our No. 1 source of excess chatter. Done right, it is an efficient and valuable business tool. But too often I have to wade hip-deep through someone's meandering before the point of the exercise even starts to become clear. I think many people treat e-mail as kind of throwaway communications, akin to opening your mouth and just seeing what comes out. That's why you see such poor sentence structure, misspellings and disorganized thinking in many e-mails. Like all good communication, e-mail must be concise and to the point.

Voice mail is one of my pet peeves. I cannot believe some of the messages I get. People ramble before they tell me what the call is about, and after I have spent several minutes listening to these messages it is hard to remember anything about them.

I had a boss years ago who told me that a quality salesperson should learn "to get in and get out" when selling something. That boss was Jim Dunn, who ought to have known what he was talking about. At the time he was the national sales director of *Life* magazine. Soon he would become publisher of *Forbes* magazine. Dunn was a stickler for good manners and not wasting people's time. He once told me that in the publishing business whenever I was selling something I should be able to give my pitch in five minutes or less. All of us should practice what we are going to say in a formal setting such as a presentation, a chat with the boss or an after-dinner speech. Say what you need to say concisely and with feeling and then stop. If someone wants to hear more about your topic, they'll ask for more.

That reminds me of a story that one of *Modern Healthcare's* best salespeople told me. One day not long after she started working here she was planning a first trip to her sales territory. I cautioned her about not overstaying the time a client was willing to give her. One of her first clients was willing to give her only 10 minutes. "I assured him I would stay only that long," she recalls. "He was obviously a very busy man, but when I started the call I told him I was new to healthcare and simply wanted to know more about his business so I could do a better job of meeting his marketing needs. He was proud of his company and he started telling me all about the products the company manufactured for healthcare facilities. As he was telling me these things I noticed the 10 minutes was up, so I started to get up. He asked me what I was doing and I explained I didn't want to overstay my allotted time. He suggested I sit down, and for the next hour and a half told me how he had started the company on a shoe-string and how lucky he had been. Later he asked me to have dinner with him and his wife, which I did."

When it comes to public speaking, brevity is even more important. Too often speechmakers don't seem to know when to end their talk. It's embarrassing and rude, and makes everyone feel uncomfortable. Really effective communicators speak concisely without a lot of excess verbiage and then get off the stage. When you see a lot of eyes drooping or people leaving, wind up the talk.

Communicating with others is an art form and needs to be perfected by anyone who hopes to get his or her ideas across. But it has to be practiced constantly, whether it's writing a letter, an e-mail or a memo, leaving a voice mail or talking in person. Be conscious of others' time and you'll win many friends and influence others more effectively than you could imagine. Be clear and concise.

Do you have the "Right Touch"?
In Sales, its essential to know how to ask for the business

Have you ever looked up the word "touch" in the dictionary? I did recently and was quite amazed at the many meanings. For instance, we've probably all heard about people who "have the right touch." How about the time we are "touched by an act of kindness." Then there's the advertising slogan that was so success-ful for so many years: "Reach out and touch someone." I'm sure we could all think of many ways to use the word. But the one I want to concentrate on involves selling.

The sales business is basically about communication between people. Some people have an ability to say and do things others just can't seem to bring themselves to do. Asking for the order is one of them. Years ago McGraw-Hill Publishing Co. did a study of successful salespeople and how many of them actually had no problem asking for business. Most of the individuals studied were seasoned pros who had been in sales for a number of years. Guess what? Only about half of them said they had no trouble asking for the order. The others admitted that for them it meant asking other people for their money, which emabarrassed them. To me that's an astounding finding. You would think asking for business would be quite routine for anyone in sales. But it isn't.

What does this have to do with touch? It has a lot to do with success in sales. Some salespeople can ask customers or clients for an order in such a way that they truly can't wait to buy. With the "soft sell" approach, there's no pressure, no strong-arm tactics, just the ability to ask for the order without offending the person you are calling on. That type of selling entails having the right "touch." But it doesn't come easy for most of us. Doing it the right way takes practice and experience, but most individuals who call themselves salespeople won't practice asking for the order. They'll practice going over promotional materials, they'll practice knowing the price list by heart, they'll even practice their presentations, but they won't practice asking for business.

That means tremendous opportunities await those willing to develop the touch.

Most of us, I believe, also want people selling to us who not only give us good service but are smart enough to play without egos. Never underestimate how important someone's ego is. We all like to be recognized, and we all love someone who takes an interest in us. The best salespeople for any organization know instinctively how to make others feel important. They take a sincere interest in the lives of their customers without being patronizing. They also don't ask for the order prematurely. They are smart enough to recognize there are good times and bad times to ask for business. They study their clients for their moods and idiosyncrasies. They do their homework on an account, and they stay in touch by "reaching out" regularly.

If you want to learn how to have the "right touch," then you have to practice the art of dealing with people. Some do it well and are very successful. They work hard at their relationships with their customers. They take nothing for granted. They stay in close contact on a regular basis, and when it comes time to ask for business they are not ashamed to do so. Most of the time they're successful because their customers respect their professionalism. They've mastered "the right touch."

WORK THE ROOM!
Salespeople need to make new contacts

Sometimes we forget. But experienced salespeople should know better. When attending any kind of social function, we need to remember how important it is to work the room. Job No. 1 is mingling with as many attendees as possible, greeting them and getting to know them better. Yet on many occasions I've seen experienced salespeople stand in one or two places talking to the same people over and over while other guests and customers are left unattended. It always makes me wonder about the training these people received.

Then there's the I'll-only-talk-to-my-colleagues syndrome. I'm sure we've all seen this happen. The purpose of these social events isn't to spend more time with your co-workers. Get out there and get to know some new people. Opportunity could be standing right in front of you. At the very least spend some time with a few of your longtime clients. Find out what's new in their lives. Selling is about relationships and schmoozing. It takes time and effort, but it shouldn't be painful. It should be fun. For salespeople who are slightly introverted, this is a little harder, but it's an obstacle that has to be overcome.

For some people, the mingling and small talk come very naturally. But that's not true for everyone. Some don't seem to have the knack for meeting people, and that's where the sales manager should come into play. He or she needs to be everyone's mentor and trainer.

If your company is hosting a social event, somebody should be standing at the door waiting to welcome guests with a warm smile and a firm handshake. Be sure your guests understand how happy you are that they are attending. But here again, too often individuals shy away from offering this simple kind of greeting. I've attended social events hosted by prominent companies in which nobody is standing at the door welcoming people to the party. Guests are left to wander into a room and find their own way. To me, that's bad manners, and it can leave your cherished guests with a cold feeling.

I know this is all very basic stuff, but far too often I see the fundamentals of sales being violated egregiously. Maybe salespeople have gotten sloppy over the years, but many times it's because they just don't know any better. And that worries me. For whatever reason, many of us are not abiding by the golden rule of sales—we must get to know our clients well and make sure they realize how much we respect them and how much we appreciate their business.

Something that continues to surprise me is salespeople forgetting to ask for the order. This can happen with rookies as well as seasoned pros. They give a great presentation about their company and their wares and then fail to ask for the business. According to some studies, the reason this occurs is because many salespeople feel embarrassed asking other people for money. If that's the case, they're in the wrong profession. And that tells you a lot about how much they believe in their products or services. They must think that they are selling something that's devoid of value. I hope that's never the case. I want to sell something that will help my customers either sell more of their own products or make them more efficient in how they do business. I want to be selling service and value. If that's not what you are selling, you probably won't be in business very long.

Another important part of this is that once you have asked for the order and have received it, make sure you thank people for their business. Maybe it's with a handwritten note or a quick phone call. You might have your own favorite ways to say thank you. The important part is to make sure you are doing it on a regular basis.

There's nothing really major here. But I urge you to take inventory at your organizations. How are you doing with the basics? Ignore them too long and it quickly could become something major. Take nothing for granted.

Overcoming sales obstacles
Sometimes you have to climb a ladder

From time to time I'm asked to speak to a sales group, and invariably my host will suggest I just pick a topic. With such groups that's easy, because I have lived and breathed sales my whole career. I can always talk about the many people I have met in this field and the stories I have heard or been a part of.

Every salesperson can tell you stories about colleagues who have overcome incredible obstacles to land an account. Selling takes courage, persistence, creativity and incredible stamina. I've seen bright, talented individuals who failed miserably at selling because they couldn't handle the 90% rejection rate all salespeople have to cope with. On the other hand, I've worked with salespeople who weren't that talented but through tenacity were highly successful. They focused on their customers, listened intently to them and did everything they could to fulfill their customers' needs and wants.

Too often, I see companies and salespeople forget what they are all about. They start taking things for granted and because of previous successes they lose their edge. Their desire to be the best fades, and they lose the desire to make that first customer visit early in the morning and the last call after 5 p.m.

There is no substitute for an in-person meeting with a customer. There's the handshake, the eye contact and the personal relationship with the customer that often develops after several such meetings. Don't count on e-mails or faxes or telephone conversations to carry the day. The face-to-face meeting is what selling is all about, and unless you are willing to pay the price to do that every day, find another line of work.

In his book *Staying Street Smart in the Internet Age*, Mark H. McCormack writes emotionally about the value and magic of personal contact in sales. His company, International Management Group, represents all kinds of sports stars and celebrities. He writes: "The Internet can't help us discover a tennis prodigy. It can't recognize talent or talk to a young athlete's parents about nurturing that talent properly. It can't help us negotiate a contract or construct a tournament schedule. That experience and judgment is the most valuable 'product' we sell in our business. And you can't learn these or for that matter, any other worthwhile interpersonal skill from the Internet. That's the big reason I feel so indifferent to both the challenge and the opportunity posed by the Internet. Our business is largely a one-on-one business. It consists of salespeople talking to customers and managers, talking to clients, each dealing with the other as an individual rather than as a community or statistic. And that sort of connection will never be threatened by the Internet."

Of course, it's not always easy to get to the person on whom you want to pay a call. I well remember being asked to moderate a panel of top executives on selling interior-design materials to hospitals. There were about 20 people involved in the meeting, and they agreed that to sell effectively to a hospital, the chief executive officer was the key person to cultivate. But it also was agreed that it was almost impossible to get CEOs to discuss such a mundane purchase.

However, as I polled each participant at the meeting about this seeming obstacle, there was a young lady sitting across from me who had introduced herself as being with a certain carpeting company. She was the youngest person there, and she said matter-of-factly that she had little trouble meeting with CEOs and had sold millions of yards of carpeting to them in her short career. I asked her how she did it. Here's her answer: "My father long ago taught me that people who run a business are usually the first ones to come to work in the morning and last to leave at night. So when I get organized in the morning I start calling at 6 a.m. And you would be surprised at how many CEOs I get appointments with. I do the same thing at night. I start calling CEOs at 6 p.m. and more often than not they are there. That's how I've been able to sell so much carpeting."

What a great example of sticking to the basics and using common sense and street smarts in the selling process. It was a magical moment. We can all learn something from this story even if we aren't in sales.

Another story I like to tell is from the publishing business. Many years ago there was an advertising space salesperson who tried for three years to get an account into his magazine. His competitor carried the regular business and the salesperson tried and tried to see the man who made advertising decisions but to no avail. Time after time he would call the executive secretary, but each time he was told the executive either wasn't in the office or was out of town. The salesman would even stop by the company when he was traveling in Wisconsin to see if by luck he could catch the gentleman. This standoff went on for three years and eventually the salesman became so frustrated he decided to do something radical. He went to find a ladder.

The company's headquarters was only two stories high, and with the help of the receptionist he found out where the executive's office was. She also tipped him off that the gentleman was in his office. The salesman figured he didn't have anything to lose so he went around to the back of the office building and hoisted the ladder up to the window. My friend climbed that ladder and there was the man he wanted to see. Now, as you can speculate, this could have gone either way, but luckily for the salesman the executive had a sense of humor and invited my friend to come around to the front of the building and visit him. The salesman got the business.

Selling is like any other discipline. Persistence and a willingness to go the extra mile always pay off. Remember the personal touch.

GIVING THAT SOMETHING EXTRA
Success is not a 9-to-5 proposition

Anyone who reads my column regularly knows I love success stories, tales about what's required to stand out in the crowd. It takes high energy, integrity, commitment and a strong work ethic, for starters. There's nothing really magical about any of those traits, since we probably all know individuals who display them on a daily basis. However, an especially important one is wrapped up in the phrase, "and then some." It's the willingness to go far above and beyond what's necessary for any job or assignment.

Most of us put in a lot of long days at our jobs and believe we work very hard. But there's something in the makeup of true winners that differentiates them from the average—they're always willing to put in the extra effort no matter what it is they're doing. It's the salesperson who stays late at the office to make a few more phone calls, because she knows many of the CEOs she needs to reach also tend to stay late. It's the individual who always takes pride in his job and is more than happy to do all the little things that others just can't be bothered with.

I have a favorite story about a Southwest Airlines employee who went out of his way to comfort a concerned passenger. The story goes like this: A woman booked a flight and also made arrangements for her dog to travel with her. She was told her pet would have to be placed in a container and travel in a special compartment in the baggage hold. When the day came to fly, the woman boarded the plane but was very concerned about her dog. Before the aircraft departed the gate, she asked a flight attendant to make sure her "baby" was on the flight and was OK. A few minutes later the attendant returned to the woman's seat and told her to look out the window. Standing below was a baggage handler holding up the container with her dog inside. All was well, and the woman was most relieved.

That story really drives home what it means to do your job and then some. What that baggage handler did certainly wasn't difficult. And it really wasn't all that extraordinary. But it sure meant a lot to that woman. For people who really love their work, the extra effort is second nature, and the employees probably feel good about it. Such an approach is also a dependable road map for success, not only for the employees but for their companies.

The sales business is another good example. Making calls on customers and prospects is the lifeblood of any successful salesperson. They do it day in and day out, but too often some salespeople cling to a 9-to-5 philosophy. They do what is necessary during regular hours but hardly ever come in early or stay late. When they're out on the road, the same rules apply. They visit a few clients, make some calls and then close up shop. But those who want to excel behave differently. They never stop thinking. They're not constantly looking at the clock. They're not afraid of overtime.

One of the most successful salespeople I ever knew was constantly in the field making calls. She made more calls than anyone in her organization, and her earnings showed it. Once she had been having a particularly difficult time with a certain account. She couldn't get an appointment to see the person who made the buying decisions, and this man had a reputation for being one tough customer. But then she finally got through to him. She had been traveling for an entire week and was looking forward to going home for the weekend. But this customer told her that the only time he could see her would be at 7 a.m. on Saturday. She took the appointment, showed up the next day on time and got the business. She could have turned down the weekend meeting, but she made the sacrifice, and it paid off.

I know it might sound like I'm saying that we should all work until we literally drop, but that's not what I'm advocating. Balance between one's personal and professional lives is critical if either is to be fulfilling and meaningful. I know individuals who have sacrificed their personal lives for professional glory and they regretted doing so later because of divorce, ill health or other factors. On the other hand, if we use discipline, it is possible to thrive in both areas. But in the work environment, there's no substitute for the "and then some" attitude. It lays the groundwork for success. Start now.

Hiring sales people
Some key traits to look for

We've been looking for a few good people recently to sell advertising space in *Modern Healthcare* magazine. Many of the candidates we have interviewed are terrific, and it's hard to decide who will do a better job. But the fun part for me is seeing who is out there and what determination and drive they have to be successful.

As you know, candidates come in all shapes and sizes and colors. Some hail from highly academic backgrounds; they are college graduates and many have gone on to do graduate work. Others haven't experienced college but still have earned degrees from schools of "hard knocks" and consequently have street smarts. I pay close attention to these candidates, because over the years I have scored some success in hiring individuals who haven't had a lot of things handed to them. They seem willing to try harder. That doesn't mean I haven't hired people with college degrees, because I have many times. But there's something about those people who have had to try harder to get where they are that manifests a strong character.

There are, of course, other things I look for. These include how someone shakes hands and whether or not he or she looks you in the eye. Both of these traits are the basis for success in sales. How can any of us trust someone if he isn't willing to give you a forthright handshake and look you in the eye when he's doing so? That's simply Lesson No. 1 in the sales handbook. But I still have people come in who offer a limp handshake and do not give very good eye contact.

Some of you might think this is all silly stuff, but if you are in the selling business, sincerity and honesty are integral to making sales. A solid handshake and straight look in the eyes convey conviction and honesty. We all look for that when we buy something, and those two traits are what I look for when I first meet a sales candidate.

Then there's the ability to communicate—in short, how one

enunciates who he is and what he stands for. Remember, the human voice is how most of us communicate with each other, whether it's saying "I love you" or "I want your business." Salespeople who cannot communicate the strengths of their companies' products and services certainly are at a disadvantage to those who can. Buyers still like to be sold to personally. Therefore, the peddler who hopes to achieve great heights in selling better should know how to articulate well. That's Lesson No. 2 in the sales manual.

Then there's dress. A big tendency in business today is to dress down. I guess everyone who supports this new fad must feel emancipated from the evils of corporate political correctness. But for a salesperson to dress down when calling on any client is the wrong thing to do. All of us should want to convey to our customers and prospects a sense of stability and maturity, and wearing a sport shirt and dungarees doesn't convey the image any of us would want when trying to make a sale. At this writing, no one I've interviewed has approached me wearing casual clothes. They are trying to sell themselves and make a good impression, and that's the way any of us should dress when we are in the field selling.

There's another important thing I look for when interviewing candidates. That is the use of one's hands. I have had prospects who are talking to me about a job literally cover their mouths most of the time so that it is hard to hear what they are saying. If you are selling to someone you want them to hear every word you are saying, and putting your hands anywhere near your face can be very distracting. Leave them on your lap or anywhere, but stay away from your face.

Then, of course, there's asking for the job. I have had a number of well-qualified individuals who looked great, had all the experience necessary for selling, yet couldn't bring themselves to ask for the job at the end of our interview. I guess they thought it is a given, but it isn't. All of us who have been around the selling business take great delight in watching young people ask for the job.

Finally, candidates who demonstrate enthusiasm when interviewing always impress me. I love to be around positive, enthusiastic people, and so do you. They energize me and make me feel enthusiastic as well, and that's the name of the game. Read the stories and observe people around you who are successful. All of them know how to make people feel positive through their enthusiasm. Be yourself.

Nuturing salespeople
Make them a top priority

The economy keeps cruising along. Some labor markets are tighter than they've been in years. That's especially true with the sales field. Quality salespeople are hard to find, yet everyone knows how critical they are to the success of an organization. Finding them, managing them and nurturing them can be difficult tasks for any executive.

Too often I see salespeople mistreated by micromanagers and so-called leaders who fail to give them the freedom and resources they need to succeed. Mentoring—or call it nurturing—is important for all salespeople, rookies and veterans alike. Even the highest achieving professionals need a coach. Every salesperson needs the total commitment of the sales manager. Yet, too often sales team members are left alone in their territories without guidance or support. Then when they resign, everyone wonders what went wrong. The reason is usually because the people responsible for supervising the sales force just weren't up to the task. But they seldom get blamed because they're most likely part of the management structure and therefore are above the fray. That's unfair.

So how do we find and keep good people? How do we make sure that after we've given them growth territories, they will want to stay? It starts when we recruit sales candidates. Too often after a territory opens up, panic quickly sets in. Management is worried that competitors will move in on top accounts, so the pressure is on to hire someone as soon as possible. "Haste makes waste" is just as true in hiring as in anything else. References aren't properly checked, and the interview process isn't thorough enough, so key questions never get asked. Are the person's skills a good match for the job? Will the person fit the company culture? Does the candidate display good manners? Is he or she a good listener? Is the person enthusiastic about the job? When the process is hurried, a lot of issues can fall through the cracks. So it shouldn't be a surprise when the person hired is terminated six months later because he or she "just didn't work out."

When you take the time to hire good people, it's also necessary to take the time to train them and manage them. Salespeople, like every other type of professional, come to the job with different backgrounds and different needs. Everyone has a different style, so using a one-size-fits-all type of management just isn't going to work. A lot of sales managers and their bosses don't understand that. They don't realize that quality salespeople are creative and competitive individuals who need plenty of latitude to do their jobs well.

I'm a big proponent of recruiting within a given organization. We should look around for good sales candidates within the walls of our own companies. Right in our own back yards are people who would consider it an honor to be invited to join the sales force. Most of these individuals already have displayed loyalty, integrity, enthusiasm and all the other things we look for in good sales candidates. However, too many managers still believe that outsiders make better candidates. Don't buy that. Try to promote from within. It's great for morale and lets everybody at the company know there is opportunity for growth. Those insiders also understand the corporate culture and are familiar with the company's products and services.

Finally, always make salespeople a top priority. Spoil them and coddle them if you have to. Spend time with them in the field. Be willing to share their joys and failures. Never take them for granted. If you pay attention and do your job, they'll repay you by giving 100% every day. That's what the selling business is all about. Be there.

Chapter **5**

HEALTH CARING

Spiritual leadership

CEOs must refocus on the reasons they got into healthcare in the first place

This magazine is a member of the Healthcare Research and Development Institute, based in Pensacola, Fla. The group includes about 40 of the top hospital and healthcare system chief executive officers in the country and many top executives of vendor companies. The reason we joined the HRDI was to get advice and counsel from the healthcare CEOs about how they are fighting to keep their organizations healthy and viable. We also want to find out if we are living up to their expectations with our information products and what new products they need to satisfy the increasing demand for information.

In the past few years, we have heard an earful. CEOs have capital access problems, personnel shortages, doctor problems. They are under a lot of stress from a variety of sources as they try to improve their business and clinical operations.

Sometimes it seems many executives take for granted what their organizations have achieved and that they are involved in one of the nobler professions, providing care for everyone in our society who needs it. This is why most executives got into the business. And that brings me to the real reason for this column.

I was lucky enough to participate in an early morning session at the spring meeting of the HRDI, one of the most stimulating and inspirational sessions I have attended. Of course, with two of the most inspirational CEOs leading the session I shouldn't have been surprised. Erie Chapman, former president and CEO of Baptist Hospital System in Nashville, has always been one of my favorites. He always has believed in treating everyone in his organization with dignity and respect. He worked with everyone from housekeeping to nurses to doctors to get a better understanding of how and what it took to perform certain duties and what might be done to make working environments better. Erie is one of those people who has never forgotten his mission—taking care of people. (He now is president and CEO of the Baptist Healing Hospital Trust.)

The other person serving as co-chairman of the meeting was Dan Wilford who retired in 2002 as president and CEO of Memorial Hermann Healthcare System in Houston. His leadership style is the same as Chapman's. He cares about colleagues and patients and is dedicated to the principles of ethics and integrity. Dan is revered by all who know him, and that is why everyone was so saddened to learn of the recent automobile accident in which his wife died and Dan was injured. He is attempting to get on with his life with the support of family and friends.

The topic of the session was "Spiritual Leadership," which is a high-minded phrase but really is simple.

You can see it in the kind of leadership practiced by Chapman and Wilford. They believe in the golden rule. They believe principle comes before expediency, and they believe the real mission of any top CEO in healthcare should be ensuring the well-being of every patient and that every other decision comes back to that concern.

Of course, there are leaders who fail to follow any of that. They simply want to dominate others. They will not abide anyone questioning their authority, and if someone does they are either demoted or fired. Other views are not to be thrown into the mix, because arrogant leaders don't care what others think or are too insecure to tolerate disagreements or the give-and-take of decision making. Everyone has been exposed to this kind of stupidity, which destroys morale.

Maybe if more people would re-evaluate the reasons they got into healthcare, they might find they have gotten off track and need to refocus. I know this only because later in that HRDI meeting the topic of spiritual leadership came up again and the response was an eye-opener for me. Many of the CEOs believed that all the leaders in healthcare spend much too much time worrying about the business side of healthcare and have lost their focus on patients. I think with all that's going on in healthcare, that isn't necessarily surprising. A CEO has to be on the ball when it comes to fiscal matters in order to keep the institution viable. But just maybe that preoccupation has swung some people too far away from the raison d'etre—patient care.

Frankly, I'm sick of hearing about things such as access to capital, or personnel shortages and compliance and all the other things that we hear about over and over these days. Of course, this magazine rightly devotes a lot of attention to those topics, but there is another aspect of running a healthcare enterprise that doesn't get nearly as much ink, and that is where spiritual leadership comes into play.

Spiritual leaders take responsibility, look out for their colleagues and lead by example, not by dictatorial orders and punishment. They don't get preoccupied by new technology that can never take the place of the human touch. They know that no machine, no technology, no new business practice or memo or regulation can replace a simple thing such as love and tenderness and a hug. I have more to say about this subject in the future, but thanks to the HRDI I was able to see a whole new side of the healthcare equation from some very caring and talented CEOs. Balance is important.

A WAKE-UP CALL FOR THE INDUSTRY
Letters from healthcare professionals highlight problems in the business

I get many letters from people who read *Modern Healthcare* and the depth of feeling of these communications always impresses me. Some of them give me ideas for future columns, while others leave me impressed with the commitment to healthcare of some of the people in our industry.

Most people I know in healthcare aren't out to make exorbitant fortunes but simply want to make a difference by helping others. That's why I feel the way I do about this field and why when asked to do so, I enjoy giving talks to healthcare groups. By the very nature of their calling, the people in this field continually inspire and motivate me.

But over the years I have noticed a shift in attitude in healthcare, and it has bothered me. I hadn't been able to put my finger on it, but I knew that something definitely had been out of whack. That's why I sat up and took notice recently when a good friend sent me an e-mail that pretty much crystalized many of my thoughts on this topic. I would like to share it with you. It's from Patrick Hays, a fellow of the American College of Healthcare Executives and the former head of the national Blue Cross and Blue Shield Association in Chicago. Today Pat serves on a number of boards and does some consulting. Pat is as bright as they come and knows healthcare cold, so when he sends me his thoughts, I pay attention to what he has to say.

"What has happened to our profession? In the pell-mell rush of the last 20 years to get 'competitive,' 'build market share' and 'kill the folks across town,' we may have lost what made healthcare management special—its sense of a higher good, of a calling. It's reflected in our vocabularies—'medical-loss ratio' for health plans, 'provider' for highly dulled clinicians; (would you want your mother or children to see a 'provider'?), 'EBITDA' or 'bottom line.'

"Here's a specific example: People! Talent, the ingredient that enables any organization to succeed and thrive. GE, Herman

Miller, ServiceMaster—they're legendary for how they treat their people. And then there's us in healthcare. In the mid-'90s we needed to 'downsize,' so many of us began by laying off RNs (note, not management). Now we wonder why RNs won't come back to hospitals. Loyalty may be an old-fashioned notion, but it's still a two-way street.

"Here's an example from an organization I know. A female exec tells a competent male manager in his mid-'50s that he no longer 'fits' with her team. No stated performance issues, no 'paper trail,' just 'hit the road, Jack' (with six months' severance). That act of wanton power has caused unwarranted pain and financial ruin to the manager and his wife, as three years later he's still searching for a full-time position. (Perhaps there is justice, though, since the exec that did the firing has also recently been 'severed.')

"I've reached the chapter in my life where I qualify for graybeard status, but I'm still quite active in our field, and I wonder where our values have gone. Do we really wonder why the media treats—and the public views—healthcare in such a negative light? Don't we really know why healthcare management's no fun anymore? Look honestly at what we have done; look in the mirror. More importantly, change it. Tomorrow morning, become a 'quiet revolutionary' and start your personal crusade to restore humanistic values alongside business acumen in the most intimate of all human services." —Pat

This letter left me thinking that maybe we have become so sophisticated in the healthcare business that we have forgotten the reasons we originally got into this field. Maybe we have become so enamored with all the wonders of corporate America that we have totally forgotten that the business of healthcare is not only about people, but also that it is entirely different from other industries.

Over the years many of us have latched onto the latest management trend, only to see it fail miserably because of the uniqueness of this field. We have become so caught up in some of these fads that we forget who and what we are. It's about saving lives, mending broken bones, making people whole again. The managers of our institutions are like symphony conductors: It's their job to bring all the disparate parts together and make the darn thing work. Too often, however, if these leaders aren't up to date on the latest management field or gimmick they feel they have somehow failed in their mission. But they haven't. Their mission is about people, not to ape what's going on in corporate America at large. Our trend should be to treat employees as well as or better than the patients, but too often in too many healthcare facilities the "help" are mistreated and abused. What kind of management is that?

Somehow, some way, this great industry has to get back on track and rekindle the flame. Get back to our roots. The knowledge and skills are there; we just need to work on the attitude.

Just last week I received an e-mail from Leonard Berry, a marketing professor at the school of business at Texas A&M University, College Station. He has just finished a sabbatical during which he studied services at the Mayo Clinics in Rochester, Minn., and Scottsdale, Ariz. Read how impressed Berry is with what he has witnessed:

"I am fascinated by the journey I am on. I am not just studying healthcare service, I am living it. Having devoted much of my career to studying corporate service, I believe I can make a contribution (by) helping business learn from healthcare and healthcare learn from business. I've been inspired by the skill, intelligence and caring of (the) doctors and nurses I have come to know and by the courage of many patients I have met."

These are just two examples of the types of missives that have inspired me. They are words we should all heed. Maybe it's time we all become "quiet revolutionaries" in our part of the healthcare world. It's a calling, folks.

LOOKING TO THE NEXT GENERATION
Healthcare executives need to help draw people to work in the industry

Spring is in the air, a time when everything seems possible. For young people, it's graduation season, as a new generation looks forward to getting out into the real world and starting careers, hoping for success and professional satisfaction. The reality, of course, can be far different. Many young people are as confused as I was when I started out many years ago, not really sure of what to do or how to get started. Even those who have a clear sense of a career path may find the job market is tight. They might have to tread water for a while doing other things to make ends meet; it can be a difficult time of life.

There are two things I preach to young people in this position. The first one applies to everybody, the second to a more select group, as I will explain.

First, no matter how tight a job market, there is always room for good people who are persistent, and that's the secret of success. Too many become easily discouraged if things don't go exactly as they anticipate. They wind up abandoning their dreams without a fight. I don't know how many times people have told me wistfully how they wanted to be a doctor or lawyer or journalist but that they didn't have enough money for school or that something happened along the way. They wind up doing something for a living that isn't what they intended, and they never get back to pursuing their dreams. So I advise them to never give up, to always keep their goals in mind as they make career or life decisions.

I was lucky—in a way. When I graduated from college I didn't have much of a choice about what I wanted to do. I was drafted into the U.S. Army to serve in the Korean conflict. That may not sound lucky, but in those two years that I was in fatigues I had plenty of time to ponder my future career. By the time I was discharged from the service I knew where I was headed, and that was into journalism. So I enrolled in the Medill School of Journalism at Northwestern University in Evanston,

Ill., to learn more about the profession. In retrospect I made a smart decision because journalism has been my career path for four decades and I have never lost my love for this great field.

No, the current economic climate isn't the best but business is starting to pick up, which will open many opportunities for college graduates. So keep dreaming.

That brings me to the second point. Whenever I have the opportunity to talk to young people, I tell them of the wonderful opportunities in healthcare administration. Healthcare may not be recession-proof, but it's as close as you can get to that ideal. As the average age of Americans rises in the next two decades, the demand for healthcare services will increase concomitantly. New healthcare facilities are going up across the country, new types of organizations are being formed, and all need someone to lead them.

When young people think about healthcare, the first thing that seems to come into their minds is becoming a physician. But not everybody has the requisite skills to be a physician or a nurse or a physical therapist. But many have administrative and financial skills, and I believe that if more young people understood the opportunities available in healthcare administration they would look more closely at the field.

What other profession does more good for mankind on a day-to-day basis than healthcare? Of course there are many well-documented problems in this industry, as any reader of this magazine knows. But from my vantage point as a journalist, I cannot think of a more honorable profession to be involved in than healthcare. Administrators may not perform surgery, but they do the work that makes cardiac surgery or neuro-oncology available to patients. They don't devise new drugs, but they run the institutions where the new drugs are administered or new devices tested. When we talk about charity care, it is administrators who do the work that makes caring for the uninsured affordable.

There is a good deal of talk today about workforce shortages, about the lack of doctors and nurses and allied health professionals. What gets less discussion is the shortage of people to run healthcare organizations, but that shortage is there, and it is becoming more acute. And what this means is that there are many opportunities out there for enterprising young people with the right kind of training.

Healthcare is like any other business, really. Unless someone is running the business properly healthcare facilities can end up closing. That has happened too many times over the past few years. Luckily healthcare has been well-served by some of the most gifted executives in American industry, and I have been lucky enough to know many of them. They are a dedicated lot, individuals who have committed their lives to serving the interests of their communities and their country. Many of them could have gone into other professions, and I'm sure done very well, but they chose healthcare.

What hasn't been done is selling the profession to young people as a place to find good jobs, and, more important, to do great things for society. I cannot think of a more fascinating, fulfilling career than healthcare administration, and I know that too many young people today who want to pursue dynamic careers don't have any idea of the opportunities that exist. We have to do a better job of finding new talent.

Good people beget good people, and I sincerely believe if more young people could spend time with current healthcare executives they would be impressed enough to choose healthcare administration as their career path. Healthcare will always need quality leadership, but we have to let people know about the challenges and opportunities that exist. Spread the word.

ONE CALL NOT TO PUT ON HOLD
*When it comes to IT, healthcare CEOs may want to hear
what experts have to say*

I was talking the other day with the chief executive of one of
the largest healthcare information technology companies. The
man seems to know his stuff, and he says he has a vision for our
industry. He told me he wants to bring order and discipline to
the business of delivering healthcare to patients. He wants every
provider to have the information systems capability to communicate effectively across the organization and with patients and
payers. He says he believes this will lead to better care for
patients and a better bottom line for providers, even if they have
to spend a lot of money to get there.

This executive impressed me not only because of his passion
but also his apparent knowledge of the industry and the trends
that are shaping it. There are some other vendor chief executive
officers whom I believe don't have a clue about the nuances of
the healthcare industry, and I always wonder how they manage to
sell their products to savvy healthcare executives. You would
think if a large portion of a company's sales is to one industry,
you might take the time to get better acquainted with what's
happening in that marketplace, but some people believe a sale is
a sale, I guess. Not true of this IT executive. He obviously has
been involved in our industry a long time.

In our conversation, we somehow got on the topic of his out-
reach to health system chief executives. Some are only too happy
to talk to him, but there are others who equate the call to just
another annoying, time-consuming sales pitch that diverts their
attention away from their jobs. Still others have made the decision to keep a closed mind about the development of new
products that may make their institutions work more efficiently
and productively on behalf of their patients.

The bottom line: My IT CEO says roughly seven out of 10
healthcare chief executives don't or won't pick up the phone, letting aides screen the calls.

I know that many executives in the healthcare world were burned in the late 1980s and early '90s by high-tech companies that waltzed in with exorbitant claims about their products that didn't pan out, costing their clients millions in the process. There may be some vendors who still don't have good products, but they are being weeded out through fierce competition. Nevertheless, I believe healthcare CEOs have to keep an open mind about all the new IT products that are being developed because some of them may be critical to the future success of their organizations. For some, IT may make the difference between winning and losing. I know that's a pretty big statement, but it seems that too many top healthcare executives aren't aware of how far behind they are in the competition. We all know healthcare has a history of failing to adopt information systems technology. In a turbulent time, when things such as electronic medical records and physician order entry may be mandated by payers, knowing all the options can only help a healthcare leader. Sure, every institution has an IT staff to talk with about this issue, but what is wrong with getting a perspective from someone at your level at a large, national vendor firm?

I know all of us in senior management are busy, but you never know when a routine call will lead to something big for you and your organization. That's why I try to answer my own phone when I can. Talking to anyone who wants to give me and my business a helping hand is always a good idea. Even if it doesn't lead to something concrete, hearing all the different ideas out there gives me perspective.

And that brings me to another point. You can't delegate all this decision-making to your IT staff or your operations people. Now don't get me wrong. If you have read this page often, you know I am a big believer in delegating authority. You have to respect your colleagues and empower them to take on the responsibility necessary to do their jobs well. You also have to listen to all of their concerns and let them play a big role in any major decision. All of that doesn't mean that you shouldn't have input from a wide array of sources before making a purchasing decision as large as a new information system, which may be the biggest capital spending deal you do during your tenure. And vendors can be sources, even if you don't happen to buy their particular product. It's part of their job to improve the knowledge base of the people to whom they market their products.

There is no question that IT can be a daunting topic and that there are many vendors in the marketplace. I also know that many CEOs think sales calls are a low priority, but it's also their job to make sure they have absolutely all the information they need to lead their organizations the right way, toward better productivity and service.

So yes, a conversation with an IT chief executive may be another form of sales call, but when an industry leader is on the line, it may make good business sense to pick up the phone and listen to someone with expertise who wants to help you. Listen and learn.

THE VIEW FROM THE TABLE
An up-close and personal look at a new surgical technique

It's one thing to talk about and report on our healthcare system, but it's quite another to be a recipient of the services the system offers. I am in the third week of recovering from hip surgery, and I have learned a few things about myself and what it means to be on the receiving end of a new surgical procedure.

Previously I wrote about meeting Richard Berger, the orthopedic surgeon who developed the new hip-replacement technique. We met on a flight to Chicago, and after hearing my tale of hip pain he opened a program on his laptop computer that illustrated his minimally invasive procedure. It was pretty amazing.

Later, my hip pain got bad enough that I asked him to evaluate me as a potential candidate for his procedure. I was scared about having surgery, but my right hip had me ready to overcome those fears. It has been bothering me for nearly three years, the result of playing ice hockey up until four years ago and years of running.

When the date for the surgery—March 26—came around, I was actually looking forward to having the hip replaced.

Berger is affiliated with Rush-Presbyterian-St. Luke's Medical Center in Chicago. His hip-replacement technique minimizes damage to muscles and tendons during surgery which leads to quicker recovery for the patient. For the past couple of decades, most surgeons favored making big incisions for hip replacement. Some made cuts 12 to 18 inches long to replace damaged bone and cartilage with a metal ball-and-socket prosthetic. Berger's technique is much less invasive: He makes two small holes in the groin and hip area—each about 1.5 inches long. He inserts half of the prosthetic into the groin, the other into the hip, putting it together at the joint.

My procedure began at 5 a.m. and took about an hour and a half. It was an exciting day, but it grew more exciting as the day went on. About 3 p.m. Berger came by my room with some

other people and suggested I take a walk with him. I was somewhat apprehensive, to say the least, but I was led down the hall
on crutches then up some stairs and down the same stairs, all the
while followed by a small entourage. I returned to my room, and
then about 7 p.m. the doctor came by to suggest it was probably
best for me to go home, which I did.

Some of the people who followed me down the hall after my
surgery were representatives of Zimmer, a company that has
worked with Berger in designing special instruments tailored to
Berger's procedure.

On average, most people who undergo this new surgery will
go home the same day. Recovery is three to four weeks. Compare
that with the traditional hip replacement, with a four- or five-day
hospital stay and three to four months of recovery, and you get
some idea of why I opted for the new technique. So far, it has
been everything it was promised to be. Just three weeks later I
was walking around without the cane. Some of my friends and
colleagues say they have never seen me stand so straight.

As I am sure you can guess, I am not the world's greatest
patient. I have had to learn patience to allow healing. Then there
is sleeping, I find it most difficult to sleep at night because I have
so much energy and have difficulty turning off my mind. Drugs
help to an extent, but I don't like getting into the sleeping pill
habit.

So as I go about my recovery, I thought it would be valuable
to others to share this experience and what I have learned. I have
had time to think about a lot of things that we don't have time
for on a day-to-day basis. The big one, of course, is the importance of family members. Their support is absolutely essential to
anyone's recovery from an illness or surgery. The other is that we
are so lucky to be in a nation where we have so many healthcare
options and dedicated physicians such as Berger who are committed to making surgery less-invasive and painful and easier to
recover from. Here's to modern medicine.

COMPASSION IN HEALTHCARE
Some institutiuons are trying harder

As I was leafing through some papers that had piled up on my desk, I came across a letter touting a book, *Radical Acts of Love: How Compassion is Transforming Our World.* Susan Skog is the author, and according to the letter she has conducted extensive research into visionary caregivers who emphasize "compassionate medicine." Even though I'd like to believe compassion should be a given in every encounter with our healthcare system, I know that's not the case.

Skog's book takes a look at the work of Griffin Hospital in Connecticut, the University of Minnesota School of Medicine, and the Center for Mind-Body Medicine and George Washington University School of Medicine, both in Washington. According to the letter, these organizations have either added compassion to their mission statements or employ caregivers who believe in the power of compassion and make it the cornerstone of their practice. As a result, the institutions have transformed medicine into a kinder, gentler and more effective endeavor. Other statements about the book suggest that throughout our culture, from community hospitals to large corporations, we've failed to solve our toughest issues when we've operated without compassion. "The idea of compassion is becoming the new vision of many institutions throughout the country," the letter states. Such comments caught my attention, especially in light of the continuing waves of layoffs in corporate America designed to fatten the bottom line.

So I read on, and through a series of stories included in the letter, I began to see what the author is talking about. For instance, at Griffin Hospital, the management team did something quite unusual to help employees see through the eyes of their patients. Employees went on a retreat at a remote convent. In a new environment, employees spent the night in a room with a stranger. There were no private baths, no room service, no TVs and no telephones. Strangers fed the employees all their meals.

The employees learned what it was like for patients to put tha trust in caregivers they didn't know

Skog's book also cites a poem that the University of Minnesota School of Medicine uses to stress to medical students the importance of compassion: "When I asked you to listen to me and you started giving advice, you have not done what I asked. When I ask you to listen to me and you begin to tell me why I should feel that way, you're trampling on my feelings. When I ask you to listen to me and you feel you have to do something to solve my problems, you have failed me, strange as that may seem. Perhaps that is why prayer works for some people, because God is mute and God does not offer advice or try to fix things. So please, just listen and hear me. And if you want to talk, wait a few minutes for your turn, and I promise I'll listen to you." As the university's Dr. Greg Plotnikoff states, "Being heard at a meaningful level can itself be profoundly therapeutic."

Then there's Dr. James Gordon, founder and director of the Center for Mind-Body Medicine and a clinical professor at the Georgetown University School of Medicine. He is an ardent believer in the power of compassion. He has used it to counsel some people from Kosovo who have been traumatized by war. He also believes in listening and the art of conversation provide the ability to "go inside the patient." His philosophy is echoed by Dr. Christina Puchalski, an assistant professor at GWU School of Medicine. "With the best technology has to offer, my patients may be cured," Puchalski says. "But in the absence of compassion, there will be no healing"

I haven't read Skog's book yet, but based on this smattering of content, I'm definitely going to. All of us seem to be in too much of a hurry these days. That includes physicians who find excuses, maybe blaming managed care or a growing administrative workload. But physicians certainly aren't alone. Too many of us just don't take the time to listen to others. Let's all try a little compassion

PROVIDING CUSTOMER SERVICE
Many hospitals don't measure up

David Zimmerman has been in the healthcare business for some 35 years. He spent 17 of those years at hospitals and has had his own consulting firm for 14 years. He recently retired as president and CEO of Zimmerman and Associates, headquartered near Milwaukee, which is now run by his son, Michael. His company advises providers, vendors, HMOs and just about any organization that needs counsel on how to improve its operations. He's also a good friend of mine. His style is direct, and he knows what he's talking about. So when he speaks, I listen.

He has published a newsletter titled *Customer Service Revolution*. If you need direction in developing a top-flight, customer service strategy, the information in this newsletter is just what the doctor ordered.

The alarming theme of Zimmerman's newsletter is that customer service doesn't get many kudos from the key audience in healthcare—the patients. Zimmerman sets the tone in the first paragraph of the issue: "The revolution for customer service has already begun. For years, Americans have told opinion pollsters that they felt disenchanted, disenfranchised and alienated from healthcare providers. Every available study indicates that patients no longer view providers as angels of mercy." That should be tough for the industry to swallow, especially for providers who think they're doing a great job serving their patients. Sure, many providers have worked hard to deliver quality service, but their customer service programs have faltered because of a lack of commitment. Customer service must be a long-term priority.

To obtain an accurate snapshot of what's happening in healthcare, Zimmerman and his colleagues talked to a broad representation of the industry, including Fortune 500 companies and managed-care organizations representing 25 million enrollees. They also conducted mail surveys and personal interviews with 2,000 patients in 17 states who had received care at 50 hospitals of all sizes. And they turned to well-known patient-survey companies, such as Press-Ganey and the Picker Foundation. Zimmerman and his colleagues found that employers are placing a higher emphasis on employee/patient satisfaction than ever before, and patients are fed up with the cold, indifferent service they encounter at hospitals and physician offices.

Here is what a few patients had to say: "They (providers) should treat you like a human being—like you matter." "Just listen to the patients. Listen to what they say, as well as what they don't say."

"Have empathy for my feelings, my confusion, my fears, my pain." Many patients also said they were treated as if they were an intrusion in a healthcare worker's day. And a maddening pet peeve continues to be the endless time spent waiting in emergency rooms, registration areas, radiology departments and doctors' offices. According to the Zimmerman data, nearly one-third of the patients interviewed or who completed a questionnaire gave their hospitals a "failing grade." The healthcare industry should be embarrassed by all of these findings.

To be fair, plenty of hospitals are dedicated to superior customer service and really do deliver on their promises. Some were singled out in Zimmerman's newsletter. One in particular, Chapman Medical Center in Orange, Calif., is feted for employing an idea used by the finest hotels. The hospital hired a concierge manager to oversee the hospital's quality of service. Debbie Firsker describes her duties: "There's one person—that's me—designated to get to know all the patients—visit them every day—make sure their needs are met, and that's all I do." Yes, Chapman is a small facility, but what the management and staff there are trying to accomplish should be the goal of all hospitals—all providers—large and small. It's essential to longevity.

Don't play the waiting game

ER should be a place where people are treated like patients and customers

In the past year, I have had way too many contacts with the clinical side of the healthcare world. I've had two hip replacement surgeries, and now my knee may need attention in the near future.

Recently an event sent me to the emergency room.

Before I go any further, I want to say my general impression has been favorable. The health outcomes seem OK, as I can now walk reasonably well. During my surgeries, just about everyone I came into contact with seemed focused and competent. The anesthesiologists, the surgeons and the nurses did their jobs well. In the ER, the care was competent.

My problem was with the customer service, or lack thereof, in ERs.

I recently needed urgent care because I was hurrying out the door to work and in my haste slammed the car door on a finger. The result was one of those cuts that you know right away needs stitches.

So off I went to my favorite hospital, relatively close to my home. I tried to reach some people I know there so I could get quicker service. I was assured someone would meet me as I entered the facility. I had no sooner entered the ER than my cell phone rang. It was my daughter, who wanted to thank me for a birthday gift. As I began to speak with her, I also heard someone tell me, "No cell phones." I couldn't very well hang up on my daughter, but before I knew it a security officer took me by the elbow and walked me outside. I was a little upset, but security is security, especially in these times, and I went back into the ER. As I entered the officer told me to sit down "in that second chair." I was not pleased by the attitude and I simply left and headed to downtown Chicago to another hospital near my office where I felt I could get decent treatment. It's a large urban institution with an excellent reputation.

Again I called ahead to the administrator's office and was told that I would be met when I arrived. That did occur and I was processed through with five stitches in my hand in about two hours. Everyone was great, including the physician who stitched my hand. I was handed a sheet of paper advising me to have the finger looked at two days later to make sure it was healing properly. I returned to work with my only real worry being whether or not I would be able to play golf over the weekend.

Two days later, however, when I returned to the same ER for that follow-up, I thought it would be quick and routine but it didn't work out that way. I had to go through a process of telling a clerk why I was there and then was advised by her to "sit down over there." I did and about 15 minutes later a nice lady escorted me to an "urgent-care center," where another woman asked for my insurance card and then spent some time getting forms together. I couldn't believe the number of forms. There must have been at least five or six of them, and she had to make copies of them, as well. When that was done, I was escorted to another area where I again was asked to wait.

To make a long story short, I never saw anybody at the hospital. I simply got up and walked out after telling one of the security people my name and why I was leaving. I waited a good hour and a half for someone to check my stitches and no one even bothered to say anything to me or the other patients who were waiting about why there was such a delay,

I finally ended up seeing my own doctor, who looked at my stitches, smiled and told me to be careful when I closed car doors. It must have taken no more than five minutes.

I'm not alone in having stories about ERs. A few years ago while playing golf with some clients the conversation got around to how long it can take before anyone gets attention in the ER. One gentleman who told his story was the vice chairman of a Fortune 500 company and chairman of a hospital board in suburban Chicago. He recounted: "I was playing tennis one day when I sprained my ankle. It hurt like the devil and I was sure I had broken something, so I managed to get to my car with the help of a friend and then I headed to my hospital. I limped into the emergency room, identified myself, gave the attendant my insurance card and then was told to sit down and that someone would be with me shortly. I sat and I sat and eventually about two hours later my ankle began to feel a lot better and I simply got up and left. I was not happy with the treatment I received and at the next board meeting I recited my story and we had a lot of discussion on emergency rooms and people kept waiting much too long."

He realized, as others have, that little things such as taking care of patients in the ER efficiently and quickly can help their institution's overall image in the community. The converse is also true, that failing to do so can result in lost market share very quickly. Complacency is a killer disease and the reason so many businesses suddenly go into a tailspin.

So while you make sure your facility provides excellent clinical care, my advice is to keep a sharp eye on how you treat your customers. Keep it simple.

IT COULD HAPPEN TO YOU

Tales of healthcare fumbling should be the exception, not the rule

I want to relate three stories that illustrate what is happening today in our industry and others. Together, these anecdotes paint a picture of poor communication, a lack of training and mentoring, low morale and just plain incompetence. These events took place at three premier medical centers in three cities, but the story is really the same in each case, and it's a sad commentary on our system of care.

The first story has to do with a top executive who one day took advantage of a free prostate-screening clinic offered at his athletic club. The physician doing the screening suggested the executive see a urologist "because there's something here that should be explored further." The man followed up with a urologist; a biopsy was taken and it was determined he had prostate cancer. He was devastated and started playing all the usual mind games. How bad was the cancer, had it spread, should he have surgery or chemotherapy? His family was distraught and so was he. But then he ran into a piece of luck. The urologist learned about a new procedure that involved removing the prostate robotically. The executive was referred to the surgeon who was performing the new procedure and after consultation, the man decided to try it.

So the surgery was scheduled and the executive was briefed on what would occur and what to expect after the surgery. Finally, the day came to go to the hospital. The delicate and complex procedure took eight hours but came off without a hitch. I have talked to the executive and he is pleased with the result, but that isn't the end of the story. After the surgery was performed, this man was put in intensive care for recovery and then moved to a private room. His wife was with him all the way, and that night in the hospital she slept in a cot in the room with him. In the middle of the night a nurse came into the room to administer a pain pill, which the patient was reluctant to take but the nurse insisted by saying, "The doctor wants you to take it." About 6 a.m. the day nurse came in to take the man's temperature and blood pressure and asked him if the night nurse had done the same tests. The answer was no. Then the nurse noticed that the drainage bag connected to the patient's incision was on the verge of overflowing. The nurse then pulled back the covers to check the calve stockings that are designed to massage a patient's legs to prevent blood clots. These hadn't been connected, and the man was lucky he didn't suffer a clot. It could have been fatal.

After only one night in the hospital the man was given permission to go home. He and his wife were told to wait for an attendant to come with a wheelchair. After a long wait, a woman attendant arrived but not in very good spirits. She kept saying things like, "This isn't even my job, but they've let so many people go recently we have to do all kinds of things that we aren't supposed to do," and, "Look what they have me doing now. I don't know what they are going to have me do next." That's the way it went until he got into his car.

So there it is. A successful surgery but the patient was lucky to have survived because people didn't do the jobs they were paid to do.

Another story I heard happened to a woman who gave birth via Caesarean section and then had to have immediate back surgery. Many doctors were involved and her husband stayed by her side for about five weeks. In a recent talk to a group of healthcare executives, he gave an emotional presentation about the experience. He actually believes if he had not been there to help he might have lost his wife. The specialists involved in his wife's care didn't communicate well, and he ended up having to coordinate everything. This failure to communicate with colleagues and associates is common in other industries as well, sometimes with disastrous results. But in medicine the lack of coordination and teamwork often means death and leaves everyone wondering whether better coordination might have saved a life.

The final anecdote involves a nurse specializing in home care. She visits all kinds of settings, including nursing homes and hospices. As I was recovering from hip surgery, she went out of her way to visit with me and offer me advice while I was recuperating at home. She did this out of the goodness of her heart; we had met only once before, and she wasn't being paid to help me. On one of her visits to my home she told me she had been diagnosed with colon cancer and would need surgery in early May. It dawned on me that here she was giving me support even when she must have been going through all kinds of mental anguish about her cancer. I told her how much I appreciated what she had done for me. She had the surgery earlier this month and so far things look promising. When I called to check on her, a friend of hers told me that when this woman arrived in her room after her surgery the bed was broken. When another bed was brought in, that, too, didn't work. Nor did a bed brought in for her friend.

You'll notice that one common theme in these stories is that each of these patients had a companion with them to help them through the healthcare process. That's a smart thing to do. But why should that be necessary? When anyone goes into a hospital or any healthcare setting, he or she should get first-class care from the administration, the nurses, the doctors and everyone else at that facility. Why are we as an industry willing to settle for less? All of us deserve better.

SAY A LITTLE PRAYER
Health benefits of faith are documented in recent scientific studies

Ernie Pyle, the legendary World Way II journalist, went into battle many times with American troops in both the Pacific and European theaters. One of the most famous quotes from his columns is, "There are no atheists in foxholes."

He understood from firsthand knowledge that when around live fire everybody, no matter how brave, is terrified that they could be maimed or killed at any moment (indeed, Pyle was killed by sniper fire on a Pacific island in 1945). Such terror isn't a sign of weakness but a basic human survival instinct. Pyle was saying that when confronted with the trauma and horror of the battlefield, praying is a natural survival mechanism for soldiers. Already there have been stories about how many of the American troops in the Middle East weren't necessarily religious at home but are praying more and attending services at bases.

I believe more people pray than most of us realize. They do so for all kinds of reasons. Sometimes our prayers are answered, and when they are we are both thankful and grateful. We are never sure how it works or precisely how to measure the psychological and physiological effects it has, but more and more studies are being done giving us some evidence that it does work.

A recent article in *Parade* magazine on the topic reminded me of a remarkable story a physician told me about a patient. The doctor had diagnosed this man with advanced lung cancer. Nothing could be done, so the man was sent home to die.

A year later my physician friend said he got a call from the emergency room at his hospital. The same patient had come in with a bad cold and was coughing quite a bit. An x-ray was done of the man's lungs and they were found to be completely clear of cancer. The physician was astounded by all this and followed up on his former patient. What he found was that when the patient had been discharged after his cancer diagnosis, the parishioners in his church started praying for him at his bedside and elsewhere. This went on for months. Eventually the patient started to improve and didn't seek medical care until he got that bad cold. The physician told me he had to attribute the patient's recovery to prayer. The doctor had become a believer in the power of prayer, even though all the proof was circumstantial.

The *Parade* article is about new research on prayer and health. In the piece, Dale Matthews, a physician at Georgetown University and author of the book *The Faith Factor*, estimates that 75% of studies of spirituality have confirmed its health benefits. "If prayer were available in pill form, no pharmacy could stock enough of it," Matthews says.

Harold Koenig, director of Duke University's Center for the Study of Religion/Spirituality and Health, says prayer "boosts morale, lowers agitation, loneliness and life dissatisfaction and enhances the ability to cope in men, women, the elderly, the young, the healthy and the sick."

A six-year Duke study of 4,000 people of various faiths, all more than 64 years old, found that the relative risk of dying was 46% lower for those who frequently attended religious services. Another study involving the same group found they had significantly lower blood pressure than the less religious. A third study showed that those who attended religious services had healthier immune systems than those who did not.

A Dartmouth Medical Center study determined that one of the best predictors of survival among 232 heart surgery patients was the degree to which they drew comfort and strength from religious faith and prayer. At the University of Miami, a research study of AIDS patients showed that the long-term survivors were more likely to be involved in religious practices and volunteer work. Another study conducted in several medical centers purports to show that prayer and faith have shown to speed recovery from depression, alcoholism, hip surgery, drug addiction and a variety of other health problems. Andy Newberg, a physician at the University of Pennsylvania and author of *Why God Won't Go Away*, has documented changes in blood flow in particular regions of the brain during prayer and meditation. He suggests, "This could be the link between religion and health benefits such as lower blood pressure, slower heart rates, decreased anxiety and an enhanced sense of well-being."

Although someone's personal prayer may help their own health outcomes, the concept of a positive effect on a person's health from the prayers of others is controversial. The *Parade* article cited studies in San Francisco and Kansas City, Mo., that found that complication rates were lower among patients in coronary-care units who were prayed for by strangers. A similar study at the Mayo Clinic found no significant benefits to intercessory prayer. But a review of 23 intercessory prayer studies involving 2,774 patients published in the *Annals of Internal Medicine* found a positive effect in 57% of the cases.

John Chibnall, who teaches in the psychiatry department at St. Louis University, is among the skeptics. "The premise behind distant healing isn't scientific. Studies cannot be designed in a scientific way," he says.

Sophy Burnham, author of *The Path to Prayer*, concedes that science may never prove that prayer can heal others. However, she adds, "That doesn't mean that people shouldn't take advantage of this wonderful tool that's right at their fingertips."

More research needs to be done, but from what I have read and heard over the years there seems to be a pretty strong case that prayer is beneficial to our health. Until we know for sure, there is no harm in trying it out for ourselves.

Chapter **6**

SINGULAR PEOPLE

A salute to Sister Irene
She was a giant in the healthcare field

How would I describe her? A good friend, a great leader, loving, gentle, full of life. Frankly, those words don't even begin to capture the essence of Sister Irene Kraus. To say she was a whirlwind would be an understatement. She was incredibly talented but humble almost to a fault. She also had the knack for always saying just the right thing. Under her genuine cloak of humility and love of mankind was a driven woman who knew how to get things done. In August, 1998, after a seven-year battle with cancer, Sister Irene finally succumbed to the ravages of that disease. She will be missed by her friends, colleagues and the industry she loved.

In March, 1998 Sister Irene attended the annual Health Care Hall of Fame festivities here in Chicago. We sat together at the dinner and talked about many things. I always loved to be with her because of her sense humor. She kidded me unmercifully, and I enjoyed every minute of it. But as she was leaving the dinner and hugs and kisses were exchanged, she said something that will haunt me forever. She said she wouldn't be with us next year. Thinking she was fatigued or just depressed, I assured her she would be attending many more Hall of Fame dinners. She obviously knew more than we did and was trying to tell us something.

Irene Kraus was born July 24, 1924, in Philadelphia to Frank and Irene Kraus. She was the third of six children. Her father was an executive with the Pennsylvania Railroad, and she obviously adored him. "My father was a very loving, fun-filled man. He loved to pull jokes on my mother and everybody else," she recalled in an interview in 1996, the year she was inducted into the Health Care Hall of Fame. "He was a very spiritual man. He would pray all the way to work. When I went with him, I would pray, too." According to Sister Irene, her mother was quite different. "She was quiet, gentle, a typical Irish person. When my brother (Frank) died (at age 23 while studying for the priesthood) of an undiagnosed condition (meningitis), my mother said that God had loaned him to us and we have to accept his decision to take him back." The influence of her mother and father gave her a superb grounding for her future.

Allow me to note a few highlights of Sister Irene's myriad accomplishments. She became the first woman chairman of the American Hospital Association in 1980. But on her election to that high office she had this to say to the AHA board: "Call me Madame Chairman. I didn't work this hard to have my title changed (to chairperson or chairwoman)." She was chairman of the Catholic Health Association in 1972 and 1973. She was the founding president and chief executive officer of Daughters of Charity National Health System, serving in the system's top job from 1986 to 1992. She described that job as the most challenging of her 14 career assignments. "We took five different jurisdictions and five different boards and got them to work as one. It was a thrill to be part of forming such a large system with high ideals." She also was awarded several honorary doctorate degrees, distinguished service medals from both the AHA and the Hospital Association of Pennsylvania, and a gold medal from the American College of Healthcare Executives.

Sister Irene was inducted into the Hall of Fame along with four other healthcare legends. Also inducted in 1996 were Edwin Crosby, M.D., executive director of the AHA from 1954 until his death in 1972; Michael Ellis DeBakey, M.D., world-renowned for his contributions to cardiovascular surgery; Walter McNerney, who served with distinction as president of the Blue Cross Association from 1961 to 1978 and merged the organization with the Blue Shield Association in 1978; and Richard Stull, who served as president of the American College of Healthcare Administrators (now the ACHE) from 1972 to 1978 and was one of healthcare's true pioneers. Sister Irene fitted in perfectly with this group. She was special.

A DOCTOR FOR THE AGES
The great legacy of Thomas F. Frist Sr.

As I began to write this column, I received word Thomas F. Frist Sr., M.D., had passed away at age 87. For those of you new to the healthcare industry, Dr. Frist was one of the cofounders of Nashville-based Hospital Corporation of America, one of the first for-profit hospital companies, now part of Columbia. But more than that he was a great leader, father, grandfather, physician, gentleman and one of the most considerate individuals I have ever known. I was fortunate enough to have been, on occasion, the recipient of his wisdom and thoughtfulness over the past 20 years. Before I learned about Dr. Frist's death, I had intended to write a column on leadership. What better example of an inspirational leader than Dr. Frist Sr. Also, what better example of an individual who put family and others above all else on life's priority scale. He practiced what he preached, reaching out in so many ways. He also was a physician's physician and a throwback to the old-fashioned general practitioner. He was a special friend, and my thoughts and prayers go out to his family,

How do I remember Dr. Frist? A few moments really stick out. For instance, a number of years ago I was visiting the HCA headquarters and had met with a number of the company's top executives. Finally, I was ushered in to visit Dr. Frist's son, Thomas F. Jr., M.D., then the company's president. We had a long and candid exchange about the future of the industry and the role of the for-profit sector. Then as we were saying our goodbyes, along comes Dr. Frist Sr., who had been on a three-day trip. As soon as Tommy Jr. saw his dad, his eyes lit up and he greeted him this way, "Dad, it's so good to see you! I just knew something wonderful was going to come out of this day, and here you are." I've always remembered Tommy Jr. saying those words because it impressed me so that a son felt that way about his father. I felt the same way about my dad and knew exactly what Tommy Jr. meant. It's special to see a father and son's love expressed openly and without embarrassment.

Then there was the time Dr. Frist Sr. was inducted into the Health Care Hall of Fame in 1990. At that time he had survived a heart attack, two bypasses, a broken neck, colon cancer and a stroke, but he was still going strong. However, because of the stroke, his speech was somewhat stilted. As he was inducted into the Hall of Fame with all the attendant fanfare, I asked him if he wanted to say a few words. He said he would but assured me it would be for only a minute since he had so much trouble articulating his words. His talk lasted for a full 15 minutes, and you could hear a pin drop in the packed hall as he talked about his family, colleagues and friends. As was his way, he attributed any success he had to others.

Another story that comes to mind was an incident during a flight to Nashville a few years back. A good friend of mine was the head of his own advertising agency in Akron, Ohio. He had a major account in the Nashville area and was on his way to make a major presentation. His flight was turned away from the Nashville airport two or three times because of fog. On the final attempt, my friend began to have a heart attack. He was in a great deal of pain, and the flight attendant got on the microphone to ask if there was a physician on board. In a moment a man came to the front of the plane and attended to my friend, who by then was lying in the aisle in great distress. After the plane landed, an ambulance took him to a local hospital with the physician from the plane at his side all the way. That evening, triple-bypass surgery was performed on the agency executive. Days later, as he was recovering, my friend learned that the doctor on the plane had been Dr. Frist Sr. That one act typified his life. He was always ready to serve others.

Finally, there's another legacy Dr. Frist Sr. leaves all of us. It's from a speech he gave in 1970: "It's not mortar and equipment that make a hospital. It's the warmth, compassion and attitude of good employees that leads to quality care." Goodbye dear friend.

CEOs HIT THE TRAIL
Increasingly, they're our visiting customers

His name is legendary. Those who knew him understood they were dealing with a consummate salesman. I had the honor and pleasure of being with him in both personal and business settings, and everything they said about him was true. One meeting with him was enough to understand what the man was all about. He was a Horatio Alger-type character who never forgot his roots. If he promised you something he never failed to deliver. He always had a smile on his face, and the people who reported to him loved him. He was the first to arrive at a party and the last to leave. His energy never seemed to give out. Frankly, I've never gotten over the guy because he was everything you looked for in a chief executive. He ran a multibillion-dollar enterprise called American Hospital Supply Co. The individual I'm talking about is Karl Bays, who to this day brings smiles and reminiscences to healthcare CEOs all over this country. He was way ahead of his time in the way he did business. He believed that the CEO of any company should, as much as possible, be in the field with customers, not sitting in the executive suite slurping coffee and dictating memos.

Although Bays died of a heart attack years ago, his example will always live on.

Bays came to mind immediately the other day when I picked up a newsletter off my desk. The newsletter reported how CEOs are becoming more active in making sales calls. The mailing came from Allen Konopacki, president of Incomm International, a Chicago-based research and sales training center. The newsletter cited a 12-month survey of more than 400 CEOs, which found that the selling process has become a bigger part of CEOs' management strategy. The findings include: 97% of CEOs say they are more active in scheduling sales calls with customers, and 53% say they visited at least three expositions in 1999. The CEOs then identified the top four venues they use for sales calls: 97% make visits to key customers' offices; 91% make customer contacts at trade shows; 79% use golf outings and other recreational events; and 51% use dinners and hospitality events.

Remember that the CEOs who responded to the survey and gave interviews come from a variety of industries and include companies with annual sales ranging from $100 million to more than $100 billion. The key point is that almost half of the CEOs—47%—indicated they spend more time supporting sales than they did three years ago. For instance, former IBM head Lou Gerstner is a great believer in being on the front lines making customer contacts. Jack Welch, former CEO of General Electric Co. is in the same category. He's in the field constantly visiting customers. The list of such active CEOs goes on and on.

I've been asked many times by representatives of great companies how they can do a better job of selling top accounts in the healthcare industry. My answer is pretty simple: Look no further than Bill Kelley, chairman of Hill-Rom Co., the top manufacturer of hospital beds. The firm holds about 90% of the bed business in hospitals and nursing homes and is considered one of the best-run companies in the country. Kelley was the leader, and he was always out there selling. That's probably one of the most important reasons for Hill-Rom's success. The bottom line: Support from the top—and better yet, a visit from the top person—gets results. Bays knew how.

FROM TRAGEDY TO TRIUMPH

Healthcare executive's story of survival serves as an inspiration to us all

Edward Eckenhoff first came to my attention a few years ago. I didn't know who he was until I read a story about him that caught my attention and earned my admiration. Since that time, Ed has been a major source of inspiration and motivation for me. There are no fluff or phony handshakes or broken promises or bandleader smiles. You see, Ed is the real article. Ed is everything that is good about life wrapped up in one precious package.

Imagine, if you will, a young man just finishing his freshman year in college at Transylvania University in Lexington, Ky. It is 10 p.m. on the last day of school and the man has retired to bed. The man's roommate arrives home after visiting his girlfriend in one of the sorority houses on campus, only to realize that he left his wallet at his girlfriend's house. The roommate wakes up the young man and asks him to join him on the drive to the sorority house.

"Join me. It will be our last ride together this year," the roommate pleads.

The young man suspects that his friend has been drinking but thinks he must be OK to drive.

Twenty minutes later, the car is upside down and off the side of the road. The roommate is dead and the young man, Ed, is lying in the middle of a cow pasture with a broken spine.

That drive was the beginning of a great saga that continues to this day, and God willing, for many years to come.

Ed's reflection on the accident and what occurred to him is noteworthy.

He makes no excuses about the fact that he was on the dean's list his freshman year, but as he puts it, he was on "the wrong one." Like so many of us at that stage in our lives, Ed lacked focus and was meandering through life without any goals or definite plan. He now believes that the tragic accident he survived was a blessing in disguise. He refers to it this way, "It was a very fortunate turning point in my life."

As a matter of fact, from that time forward Ed Eckenhoff has never looked back and has managed to accomplish things that others only dream about. He earned his bachelor's degree from Transylvania, a master's degree in education from the University of Kentucky and eventually another master's degree, this one in healthcare administration, from the Washington University School of Medicine in St. Louis.

He has done more than dream his dreams; he has made them a reality through his enormous courage, persistence, drive, integrity and ingenuity. But he hasn't been alone.

One of Ed's brothers is a world-renowned architect who has designed a number of hospitals and healthcare facilities and now is designing a home for Ed and his wife in Naples, Fla., for when Ed decides to "come off the field of play."

Ed's youngest brother is one of the top anesthesiology scholars in the country, doing work at the University of Pennsylvania Medical School.

Ed lost his twin brother years ago to acute lymphatic leukemia. Before his death, he enjoyed a distinguished career as a research entrepreneur. His most famous invention, "the patch," is used for all kinds of products. Before his passing, Ed's brother had more than 100 patents to his name.

Ed has mentioned how important his father was; he was a role model for Ed and his brothers. He served as dean of the Northwestern University's Feinberg School of Medicine for many years and had distinguished himself as a renowned medical educator and scholar. Ed's dad passed away two years ago.

Then there's Judy, Ed's wife, whom he met when he was the administrator of the Rehabilitation Institute of Chicago, At the time, she was the supervisor of the occupational therapy department. They dated for a couple of years and eventually married. Anyone who has ever had the pleasure of observing them at a social occasion knows that theirs is a true love story that grows stronger as the years pass.

After their marriage Ed was approached about developing a world-class rehabilitation hospital in Washington. The rest, of course, is history.

Ed Eckenhoff has made his dreams come true. The National Rehabilitation Hospital is a model of excellence and ingenuity recognized all over the world, and the person responsible for its birth and growth is one of the most admired individuals in healthcare—Ed.

I asked Ed what his formula for success is, and this is what he told me: "We all have dreams, and I believe it is important to make them come true. But in order to make dreams come true, you have to adjust your own thinking and accept others' ideas and thinking so they accept what you are trying to do." The other thing he made clear was that even though the National Rehabilitation Hospital is successful, he and his colleagues are always on guard against complacency.

That's good advice for all of us. A turning point can come at any time.

GLAD THIS DOCTOR IS IN

NIH's Zerhouni an example of unconventional leadership that works

People often ask me where I get ideas for this column. Many come from my experiences and others from things I have read. Every day I read books, magazines and newspapers. We are lucky in this nation to have such great magazines and newspapers, but too often I hear that people don't take the time to get much past the headlines, if they read at all.

Two of the newspapers I make an effort to read every day are *The New York Times* and *The Wall Street Journal*. Recently, the *Times* published an interview with Elias Zerhouni, director of the National Institutes of Health. Normally, I wouldn't expect to be mesmerized by such a Q-and-A, but as I read this interchange I became quite intrigued.

Maybe that's because I always am impressed by leaders who espouse management tenets that are a little out of the ordinary and reveal empathy and sensitivity, traits missing in many leaders. Too often people are put into top posts because they have an outstanding sales record or are bean counters who know more about cost cutting and busting people's careers than about the core values of the business.

Zerhouni was born in Algeria and came to this country in 1975 after graduating from medical school at the University of Algiers. The article points out that Zerhouni has been a "researcher, an inventor, a businessman and a professor of medicine." Before coming to the NIH he was executive dean of the Johns Hopkins University School of Medicine in Baltimore and chairman of the radiology department there.

He was asked by the *Times*: "You've been head of the National Institutes of Health for a year now. What is your job? Are you a politician? A scientist? A manager? All of those?" He replied: "First of all I come to it as a scientist. Disease knows no politics. And science advances in ways that are unpredictable. I think it's very important for scientists to be in leadership positions to inform, to enlighten the debate, but also lead the debate as to what are the best pathways for reducing the burden of disease."

When asked, "What does it take to be a leader?" he said, "I think there are three things. First, you have to have a big heart. Because if you don't have a big heart you will never be able to lead, and a big heart means several things to me. You have to have a passion. You have to believe in some things that are your core values. The second is you have to have a spine, which means stand up for what you think and take risks that you think are important. And the third and least important is brains. People often think that high intelligence is a prerequisite. I don't believe so. I think a big heart and strong spine are more important than high intelligence."

I've never met Zerhouni, but what he had to say—not only about the mission of the NIH and leadership—is good common sense, something that seems to be in short supply these days as you watch the performance of many so-called leaders running all kinds of organizations.

Another part of the interview that caught my notice had to do with recruiting good scientists to the NIH. Zerhouni makes it clear that recruiting people into government is difficult because the rewards and fringe benefits in the private sector often are more rewarding. When he first came to the NIH there were six research vacancies. Asked how he made a specific hiring decision to fill one of those posts, he said: "Dr. Tom Insel ran the primate research center at Emory (University in Atlanta). When I went down there I spent time with him to try to get a sense about his vision, and how he managed people. Scientifically, he was strong. And then I came to a room where he introduced me to his lab, his postdocs. It was a beautiful room, and I said: 'Well, you all are very well-treated around here. This is your lounge.' And then they told me: 'Oh, but you know, this wasn't our place. This was supposed to be Dr. Insel's office, and he gave it to us.' And I went to his office, and his office was like a little corner. I said, 'That's the man I want.' "

At the end of the *Times* interview, Zerhouni's humility and candor came through loud and clear when he was asked, "Does being from another country influence your work?" He answered, "You want to pay back. I think America treated me well, and I think you have to be grateful and have a sense of duty. Also, when you leave your country you take a chance, so there is a natural selection here that's ongoing: I'm not risk-adverse. Taking risks is part of leadership. Some people ask me, 'What did you think about this? You're an immigrant, you're not born here, you've come through the ranks at Hopkins and then you're picked at NIH.' I say, 'Look, it says more about America than it says about me.' "

Zerhouni did what so many people have done in coming to America to fulfill his dream. Here you can find the opportunity to be whatever your skills and effort allow you to be.

In the good doctor's case, it meant becoming the leader of a key healthcare institution. Perhaps the doctor would not have had such an opportunity elsewhere, especially as an immigrant. I am glad he did follow his dream. We need more leaders like him. The doctor knows best.

A TRUE WINNER

One man's exhilarating journey through life

Life is funny, isn't it? It's so easy to overlook some of the most wonderful things that go on around us. We get caught up reading about events happening in another part of the country or another corner of the world. But if we pay attention and take the time to listen, we'll realize that there's plenty happening in our own communities.

I'd like to share one of the most inspiring stories I can think of, and it involves someone I've known for years. This individual lives in my hometown and is one of the most professional, successful, ethical salespeople I've ever known. You could say he is a legend. His name is Theodore Burke, and he worked for the McGraw-Hill Publishing Co. selling advertising space in the respected journal *Postgraduate Medicine.*

I knew Ted for decades since we shared an apartment in St. Louis when we were both beginning our careers. At that time he worked for the *Saturday Evening Post* and I worked for *Life* magazine, then two of the most-respected publications in the world. After a year or so of rooming together, Ted went his way and I went mine, and it was many years before I saw him again. When I did, he was a volunteer coach for the lightweight football team (for 12- to 14-year-olds) my son was playing for. My son, Randy, thought the world of Coach Burke. And one year Ted and the other coaches led the team to a state championship. It was really something.

Although he was involved in football and I coached in the local hockey program, both of us were so busy with our families and careers that we rarely saw each other. But I did hear news about Ted now and then because we were in the same business. One of my favorite stories involves the time a top McGraw-Hill executive came to Chicago to discuss the company's retirement program. Apparently the meeting went on much too long. Finally, in exasperation, Ted stood up and said something like, "If you don't mind, I would like to excuse myself from this meeting.

I have to get back to my job of selling advertising." In short, Ted Burke has always been a salesman's salesman.

A couple of years ago I heard more news about Ted, but this time it wasn't all good. Although he had become an avid runner and was in great physical condition, without any warning his kidneys started to shut down. Dialysis and a kidney transplant followed. In the course of all this he contracted meningitis. Then came prostate cancer and shortly thereafter a heart attack. Then, as a result of the X-rays from his heart treatment, doctors found a spot on one of his lungs. It was biopsied and determined to be malignant. Part of a lung was removed. He didn't let all the terrible diagnoses and setbacks deter him from the job he loved. It's amazing what he endured without throwing in the towel.

I called Ted to see how he was doing. He was upbeat and full of enthusiasm. We talked about a number of things, including his lovely daughters Kelly, Megan and Tracey and son Michael. Michael has followed in his father's footsteps and sells advertising space for *American Druggist*. And among other things we talked about his philosophy of selling: "It's a great profession for anyone who doesn't have an ego problem. You can't take rejection personally. If you do this isn't the business to be in. You know I still get a rush from selling a quarter of a page or a full page. It's the greatest feeling." I also asked him about retiring. "Marilyn (his wife) has talked to me about it!" But then he laughs, and you know he isn't going to retire.

Ted Burke was in my personal Hall of Fame for years—and still is, although, sadly, he passed away in 2002. I admired him for his tenacity. Some people talk the talk, but Ted walked the walk. He was the epitome of courage and persistence.

Two amazing nonagenarians

Reflections on Peter Drucker and Micheal DeBakey

These are amazing times. People are definitely living longer, and a couple of individuals with the most brilliant minds of the 20th century are still productive and contributing intellectual riches to mankind long after others would have chosen retirement. Both are in their 90s.

They are Peter Drucker and Michael DeBakey, the famed heart surgeon who revolutionized heart surgery and is a member of the Health Care Hall of Fame. The wonderful thing for me is that I've spent some time with both individuals. In fact, a few weeks ago I had the pleasure of having dinner with DeBakey at the American Institute of Architects Academy of Architecture for Health Design awards presentation in Houston. At the event he was feted for his incredible contributions to healthcare, and a special award was named in his honor.

My encounter with Peter Drucker took place in Claremont, Calif., several years ago. He was a professor in residence at the Claremont College business school. I had been asked to moderate a healthcare CEO conference sponsored by Baxter and ServiceMaster. It was an unexpected honor, and I looked forward to meeting a man who had been one of my heroes for years. The night before the opening of the seminar there was a get-acquainted dinner, but Drucker didn't appear. So the next day when I introduced him to the gathering of about 75 CEOs, I hadn't had an opportunity to talk to him and ask what he wanted me to say. When it came time for him to speak to the CEOs I simply said: "This man needs no introduction. He is an icon and legend in his own time, Peter Drucker." Well into his 80s, he briskly strode to the front of the room and then delivered one of the most riveting monologues I've ever heard. The audience was spellbound.

According to an article in *The New York Times*, Drucker hasn't slowed much. Over the course of his career he has written some 31 books. His latest work is titled *Management Challenges for the 21st Century* (HarperBusiness). *The Times* article takes a close look at Drucker's view of the corporate mind-set: "For his part, The Man Who Invented Corporate Society (a biographer's apt label) disdains a corporate order that is in thrall to stock prices and that rewards its chief executives as though they were power forwards. 'Earnings per share' does not exist in Peter Drucker's vocabulary. The religion of shareholder supremacy has him shaking his head." Then there's a quote from Drucker: "That's right, I am not very happy with the unbalanced emphasis on stock price and market cap and short-term earnings. The most critical management job is to balance short-term and long term. In the long-term, today's one-sided emphasis is deleterious and dangerous."

The interview with Drucker makes it clear he believes customers and highly skilled employees are at least as precious as investors. Therefore, according to the article, increasingly, as pension beneficiaries, owners of stock options or mutual fund investors, they are one and the same. Learning to balance these divergent but shared interests is "the challenge of the next 10 years," Drucker says.

DeBakey is in the same league. Back in 1964 he performed the first successful coronary bypass surgery, a procedure that has become almost routine for millions of Americans. When Russian President Boris Yeltsin was having heart problems a few years ago, DeBakey was brought in as a consultant. And ever since the '60s DeBakey has had a hand in training just about every vascular surgeon in this country.

Drucker and DeBakey personify the words "total dedication." Age really is relative.

A PROFILE IN COURAGE
Legislator's speech a reminder of early lessons about racial equality

Many years ago when I was a high school student in Buffalo, N.Y., my mother and father lived in the Fairfax Hotel, which had many permanent guests. Living in a three-room suite was a little cramped with two adults and a young man who was full of energy, but we all survived, and I remember with some fondness many of the people I came to know in the hotel,

One was Al Clark, a bellhop. He was very athletic and always was in great spirits. When my parents would go out for the evening, Al would sometimes stay with me, and as a result we became good friends. When I played high school football, he never missed a game. After the game, Al would tell me what I did wrong and what I did right. There were many times I would ask him to help me with my homework and he always would comply. And because my dad traveled so much, in many ways Al served in that capacity and always was there to guide me. I never for one minute thought about his being black or that his guiding me through my teen years was anything unusual. Al Clark shaped how I felt about a lot of things, and it wasn't until I was older that I realized how much he contributed to my life.

That may be why I am always surprised at the way people have to be told they should feel good about the diversity of our culture. I have always felt that our mix of races, religions and ethnicities is the backbone of this great democracy. People should he judged on their merits as people and not on the color of their skin or their religion. When I see prejudice, I am both disappointed and disgusted.

While traveling recently on a plane from Chicago to Fort Myers, Fla., to attend a healthcare think tank, I read an account of a great event in recent history, one you may not have heard about. The hero of the story is Dan Ponder, a businessman and former Georgia state legislator who was a recipient of the John F. Kennedy Profile in Courage Award in 2003.

In 2000, the Georgia Legislature was debating a hate-crimes

bill. At that time it looked as though the bill would be defeated easily. Then Ponder, at that time a Republican representative from a rural, conservative district in southern Georgia, rose to speak. I would like to share his words with you:

"I am probably the last person, the most unlikely person, whom you would expect to be speaking from the well about hate-crime legislation.... I am a white Republican, who lives in the very southwest corner of the most ultraconservative part of this state.... I was raised in a conservative Baptist church. I went to a large, mostly white Southern university. I lived in and was the president of the largest, totally white fraternity on that campus. I had nine separate great-great-great-grandfathers who fought for the Confederacy.... And it is not something that I am terribly proud of, but it is just part of my heritage, that not one, but several of those lines actually owned slaves.

"There was one woman in my life who made a huge difference, and her name was Mary Ward. She began working for my family before I was born. She was a young black woman whose own grandmother raised my mother. Mary, or May-Mar as I called her, came every morning before I was awake to cook breakfast so it would be on the table. She cooked our lunch. She washed our clothes.

"But she was much more than that. She read books to me. When I was playing Little League, she would go out and catch the ball with me. She was never, ever afraid to discipline me or spank me. She expected the absolute best out of me, perhaps, and I am sure, even more than she did her own children. She would even travel with my family when we would go to our house in Florida during the summer, just as her own grandmother had done.

"One day when I was about 12 or 13, I was leaving for school. As I was walking out the door she turned to kiss me goodbye. And for some reason, I turned my head. She stopped me and she looked into my eyes with a look that absolutely burns in my memory right now and she said, 'You didn't kiss me because I am black.' At that instant, I knew that she was right.

"I denied it. I made some lame excuse about it. But I was forced at that age to confront a small dark part of myself. I don't even know where it came from. This lady, who was devoting her whole life to me and my brother and sister, who loved me unconditionally, who had changed my diapers and fed me, and who was truly my second mother, that somehow she wasn't worthy of a goodbye kiss simply because of the color of her skin. ... I am not a lawyer. I don't know how difficult it would be to prosecute this or even care. I don't really care that anyone is ever prosecuted under this bill. But I do care that we take this moment in time, in history, to say that we are going to send a message ... to people who are filled with hate in this world, that Georgia has no room for hatred within its borders."

After the speech, the Georgia House erupted in applause from legislators of both parties and passed the hate-crimes bill. True courage.

MIRACLE MAN

Herb Brooks lived a life that inspired others to achieve their dreams

Do you believe in miracles? I sure do. Anybody who has been around healthcare for very long knows miraculous things occur every day in our healthcare institutions: premature infants who survive incredible odds and develop into healthy human beings; complicated, lifesaving surgeries; dedicated nurses and rehabilitation professionals who help people recover after horrific accidents. Sometimes, I'm afraid we take a lot of these things for granted, but we shouldn't. We should be grateful for these gifts.

The reason I bring up the subject of miracles is because of the death in 2003 of a sports icon in a car accident. His name was Herb Brooks and he was very involved in another kind of miracle at the 1980 Winter Olympic Games at Lake Placid, N.Y.

The U.S. Olympic hockey team's gold medal performance at those games became known as the Miracle on Ice and was called the greatest sports moment of the 20th century by *Sports Illustrated*. For those who are too young or not sports-minded here is why a hockey victory was so important: A team of amateurs—a bunch of college kids, really—beat an absolutely brilliant professional hockey team from the Soviet Union that had been heralded as one of the greatest teams of all time. A week before the Olympic competition, the same Soviet team had beaten the American team, 10-3, at Madison Square Garden. The nation was depressed over the Iran hostage crisis and a myriad of other problems once described as "a national malaise."

Brooks was the coach of the young U.S. team. He was a genius of sorts who applied various psychological techniques to motivate his players and make them believe in themselves. His story is as American as apple pie and that's what makes his untimely death even sadder.

In the earlier loss to the Soviet team, Brooks saw something that made him believe his team could win at the Olympics. He thought the Soviet players were going through the motions. Yes, they were skilled, smart and experienced, but they played without passion.

Brooks' goal was to persuade his players that with the right attitude and energy, they could defeat the Soviet squad. He kept telling his players that playing with heart could be the difference between winning and losing, even against superior talent.

We've all seen individuals and even organizations like that Soviet team, doing what it takes to get by, showing no enthusiasm, commitment or love of work. We also have seen what can happen if an organization has heart and teamwork and a commitment to excellence.

When Brooks saw what was happening with the Soviet team, he drilled it into his players day after day that they could win. He believed in a dream and made the Miracle on Ice come true.

Brooks was raised on the east side of St. Paul, Minn., a blue-collar, lunch-pail community. All of his friends agree that he never forgot his roots and visited often.

Before coaching the 1980 Olympic team, Brooks became a Minnesota icon by leading the University of Minnesota to National Collegiate Athletic Association hockey titles in 1974, 1976 and 1979.

When he took over the Minnesota program in 1972, it was in shambles. After the Olympics, he would coach four National Hockey League teams, guide St. Cloud (Minn.) State University through its transition from a third tier to first division college team and coach the 2000 U.S. Olympic hockey team to a silver medal.

Along the way, he never compromised his values and principles. Glen Sonmor, his former coach, who had recruited Brooks to play at the University of Minnesota, said this about Brooks: "He made an impact like no one else. He was a person of convictions and character who wasn't afraid to take an unpopular stand and stick up for what he believed in. He was one of a kind."

Early in his life Brooks understood what disappointment could do. He was the last player cut from the 1960 Olympic hockey team. That didn't stop him from making the 1964 and 1968 teams. The disappointing moment in 1960 probably helped shape his intense, competitive personality.

You may wonder why I would write about a hockey coach in a healthcare magazine read by so many sophisticated leaders. It's because I believe Herb Brooks is what leadership, passion, focus and dedication are all about. Brooks deserves special recognition because he was instrumental in bringing us one of the greatest moments in U.S. sports history at a time when we needed a lift. His life and work provide an important lesson that goes beyond sports. Herb Brooks personified the American spirit. Stubborn, giving, passionate, committed, focused and determined. Daring to dream of seemingly impossible achievements. Making those dreams come true.

Some time after his Olympic success Brooks described himself, "I'm still driven by these same dreams. I'm driven by the pursuit of perfection, as opposed to the quick-fix mentality that I think has engulfed our society today. I'm probably a dreamer more than anything else." Believe in miracles.

FAREWELL TO CHARLES SCHULZ
'Peanuts' creator's own story was one of perseverance

When I heard about the death of Charles Schulz, it was as if I had lost a good friend. I'm not an avid comics page reader, but I did read "Peanuts" from time to time. There was a lot about that gang that I admired. First of all, even though Charlie Brown never seemed to grab the brass ring, he never let it deter him. He kept plugging along. I loved his tenacity and heart. Then, of course, there was Snoopy. He was a dog that obviously never thought of himself as a dog. I'm a bona fide dog lover, and Snoopy reminded me of so many canines I have either owned or met over the years.

According to the obituary in *The New York Times*, "Peanuts" was read by 355 million worldwide. The timing of Schulz's death from a heart attack was almost mystical, since his death coincided with his last strip. That strip carried these words: "I have been grateful over the years for the loyalty of our editors and the wonderful support and love expressed to me by fans of the comic strip. Charlie Brown, Snoopy, Linus, Lucy ... how can I ever forget them."

Lynn Johnston, a friend of Schulz's and the creator of "For Better or for Worse," told the Associated Press: "It's amazing that he dies just before his last strip is published." Then she conjectured that such an ending was "as if he had written it that way." She went on to talk about something Schulz had told her recently: "You control all these characters and the lives they live. You decide when they get up in the morning, when they're going to fight with their friends, when they're going to lose the game. Isn't it amazing how you have no control over your real life?"

"Peanuts" reached readers in 75 countries, appearing in 2,600 papers in 21 languages. It also made Schulz very rich. The comics, merchandise and product endorsements brought in $1.1 billion per year. It was reported that Schulz made $30 million to $40 million annually. Schulz was a genius, and his saga of the "Peanuts" characters was "arguably the longest story ever told by one human being," stated Robert Thompson, a professor of popular culture at Syracuse University.

"Peanuts" and Charles Schulz were totally intertwined. Schulz's personal story is one of perseverance. Out of calamity and disappointment came unbelievable success. Some things that happened to him in his early years provided the backdrop for his cartoon strip. For instance, at Central High School in St. Paul, Minn., he flunked Latin, English, algebra and physics. The cartoons he drew for his high school yearbook were rejected. But the cruelest rejection happened later while he was an art school instructor. He fell in love with a redhead named Donna Johnson and proposed marriage. But she turned him down. Schulz never forgot her. She became the Little Red-Haired Girl, Charlie Brown's unrequited love, who was often referred to but never appeared in the strip. In his 1980 book *Charlie Brown, Snoopy and Me,* Schulz affirmed what many talented writers and poets have discovered during their careers: "You can't create humor out of happiness." His basic philosophy of "Peanuts" was that "all the loves in the strip are unrequited; all the baseball games are lost; all the test scores are D-minuses; the Great Pumpkin never comes; and the football is always pulled away." But everyone carries on.

His second wife, Jeannie, claimed that all the characters in "Peanuts" were parts of her husband. "He's crabby like Lucy, diffident like Charlie Brown. There's a lot of Linus—he's philosophical and wondering about life." According to the *Times* obituary, Schulz was a melancholy man who was often worried, lonely and bitter. He had a white terrier named Andy and played golf, tennis and bridge. His greatest loves were ice hockey and ice skating. In fact, every year he hosted a major amateur hockey tournament with teams coming from all over the country to compete.

Schulz had great love for the little guy and animals. He once stated that his philosophy of life could be found in the verses of St. Luke: "It were better for him that a millstone were hanged about his neck, and he cast into the sea, than that he should offend one of these little ones." I know all of us will miss the little ones like Lucy, Linus and Snoopy. So long Charlie.

SHE'S ONE IN A MILLION
In praise of Cathy, his right-hand woman

Frankly, I couldn't do without Cathy. She's everything to me—administrative assistant, organizer, psychologist and dear friend. Professional Secretaries Week is coming up, and I can't think of anyone who deserves recognition more than Cathy. When she's not around to keep me on track, I become unglued. She's honest, she's direct and she's a class act. I get compliments all the time from people about her good nature and unfailing willingness to help. She also has a lot of old-fashioned girl in her. Her husband, Michael, and her Yorkshire terrier, Rocky, are her life. There isn't a day that goes by that I don't hear some new saga about Michael and Rocky. I just love those stories.

Cathy started working at Crain Communications when she was 16, so she's been with the company for more than two decades. We joined forces more than 10 years ago, but at first I thought she was a little too shy for the job. As the months passed, she seemed to become more comfortable and assertive. Today I couldn't think of a better match.

But what really sticks in my mind from those early days was how much Cathy adored her father. He had become quite ill and eventually had to undergo a number of complicated tests. Because her mother had passed away some years earlier, Cathy would spend long evenings with her father after working all day. This went on for months, and I watched with sadness as her dad continued to fail and then passed away. I was able to identify with her because I had lost my dad a few years earlier. Those were tough times for Cathy, but she gave her job 100% every day.

Cathy has learned to never give me an original of anything. In fact, she usually makes four or five copies of any correspondence and then gives me one, along with an admonition that I'd better not lose it. Invariably I do misplace it. But Cathy seems to have a magic touch. I've seen her sift through piles on my desk and in seconds find something I've been trying to locate for days.

There are other things, of course, that mystify me. She seems to read my mind when it comes to scheduling a trip or arranging a meeting. By the time I get around to telling her what I want to do, she already has arranged flights, hotel rooms and all the other things that need to be done for a successful trip. She's always there when I need her but never makes a big deal of it. The expression "steady as a rock" comes to mind.

When Cathy takes a vacation, I just hope I can get through each day without doing something foolish, like scheduling two or three lunches on the same day or agreeing to a speaking engagement in one part of the country when I'm scheduled to be in another part. It's happened. She's also a master at reminding me about important things like birthdays and anniversaries.

What does it all boil down to? I'm just plain lucky, the way I see it. And I know many of you have the same feelings about someone you work with, someone just like Cathy who you can trust at all times. They're the ones who keep the stress level at low tide and who really keep things running.

So Cathy, thank you for just being you. I know Michael and Rocky are just as proud of you as I am. You're one in a million! Indispensable is the word.

Chapter 7

ETHICS

INTEGRITY IS EVERYTHING
Without it, a company is doomed to fail

I was recently asked to speak to a group of 12 chief executive officers. They have formed an alliance that allows them to talk to each other regularly and pick one another's brains regarding problems they encounter in their day-to-day operations. They meet one morning each month and have a retired CEO serve as their ad hoc chairman. It was fun being with them, and the discussion at one point turned to business ethics. They talked about issues like keeping promises, making sure customers are treated right, and being forthright with employees. It was a far-ranging discussion, and I was impressed by the candor of the executives.

At one point I was asked what I think about members of generation X and how they function in the workplace. Did I think they are as loyal, honest and hard-working as previous generations? They were tough questions, and my response was direct. I said I think they are honest and hard-working, but in general, I think they may be less loyal than older generations. They don't seem to have the same commitment and dedication as some of their older colleagues. I think they approach their jobs with a different set of attitudes. If they are interested, they work just as hard as anyone else, but keeping them challenged can be tough. They definitely need the right kind of leadership.

Then one CEO brought up another tough topic: integrity. That discussion has kept coming back to me for the past few days. Integrity from my point of view is another word for honesty. It's also part of the ethics equation. It's keeping your promises to your colleagues and customers. It's always playing square. It's not running away from responsibility. Unfortunately, I hear stories every day about companies that don't keep their promises and seem to believe that promises, like rules, are meant to be broken. One supplier I know struck a deal with a certain client and then went down the street and signed another deal with the client's No. 1 competitor. When confronted, the supplier's top executive said to one of the chagrined customers: "I

didn't think it would bother you." Later the supplier was bought
out by another organization, but the execs never bothered to
inform their customers. Consequently, a number of clients fired
the firm, and no one could persuade them to come back. So
much was lost just because the company wasn't upfront with its
most important asset—its customers.

Maybe all this is a sign of the times. Greed is probably part
of it. But just about every day I hear someone say: "You know,
not too long ago we simply shook hands and kept our promises."
Today, however, papers have to be signed, lawyers are all over the
place, and it seems nobody trusts anybody. We all pay a price for
the unscrupulous operators.

Let me tell you what I told a group of salespeople at their
national sales meeting recently. People buy from a certain salesperson because they believe in that person's integrity. Integrity is
the backbone of any company or organization. Without it you go
out of business. If a salesperson breaks the bond of trust, something very sad happens. He or she loses the one thing that
matters the most. Losing your integrity is like losing your heart.
How about companies that literally sell out to another outfit and
don't take care of their employees, many of whom have been
with them for years, in good times and bad. But you can bet the
executives will make sure they escape unscathed with their golden
parachutes. Come to think of it, maybe that's the reason so many
in the younger generations are so cynical. They've learned by
observing unseemly corporate behavior. Healthcare certainly has-
n't been immune to these failings.

Integrity is only a word to many people, but for anyone in
business it should be the cornerstone of the operation. It will set
you apart from the rest. It shows.

TRUST MATTERS

We need to know we can count on others

The title is intriguing: *Trust Matters*. It's a book written by two healthcare professionals, Michael Annison and Dan Wilford. Annison is president of the Westrend Group, a consulting company based in Denver. His first book, *Managing the Whirlwind: Patterns and Opportunities in a Changing World*, won the American College of Healthcare Executives' 1995 James A. Hamilton Award as "The book of exceptional merit in the field of healthcare or general management." He knows healthcare well. Wilford retired in 2002 as president and chief executive officer of Memorial Hermann Healthcare System in Houston. He's been a respected leader in healthcare for years. In March 1997 he received the ACHE's Gold Medal Award as the nation's outstanding healthcare executive. These two savvy individuals offer one of the best treatises on leadership I've read in some time.

The authors start by telling us why trust matters in the healthcare industry. They offer four reasons: "First, trust matters because we have exhausted the benefits of existing management theories about how we should treat each other at work." They argue that healthcare executives in many cases have adopted management theories from other industries. However, in doing so they have gotten away from focusing on people and instead have become infatuated with things like specialization, impersonal decision making and hierarchical controls. "Second, trust matters because tidy organizational charts on their own won't enable us to accomplish what we need to do," the authors say. A lot of the organizational experimentation has delivered less than was expected.

"Third, trust matters because it affects how we manage people." Simply ordering people to do certain things doesn't really cut it anymore. True leaders have to capture the hearts and minds of their colleagues so they are committed to a goal. "Fourth, trust matters in the relationships between healthcare professionals and the people they serve." Trust is important because patients think it's important. Countless cases of healthcare fraud and HMO horror stories have diminished trust in the industry.

Annison and Wilford then outline the seven elements of trust. They start with commitment. "We trust people who understand the meaning of commitment, and whose actions make it clear they are committed to something more than themselves." Familiarity is next. "We trust people and institutions when we believe we know them well enough to know they can be trusted." Then there's personal responsibility. "We trust people who are willing to take responsibility for their behavior." That's followed by integrity. "We trust people who are honest." They say a second aspect of integrity involves self-awareness—in other words, what you stand for and care about. Consistency is the next element. We all like people we can rely on, no matter what the circumstances. Communication and forgiveness/reconciliation follow. Open communication is essential to trust. And the willingness to forgive and forget also has its place in the equation. How can we get on with our objectives if we hold grudges?

The final element underlying the concept of trust, according to Annison and Wilford, is understanding that the essence of trust is spiritual and requires faith. "Spirituality provides the basis for trust because it compels us to consider the morality of what we do."

Trust is critical in any relationship. None of us likes to work with people who can't be counted on. None of us likes to do business with organizations we don't believe are playing fair. Trust is the backbone of democracy. It's a tenet of being a decent human being. Unfortunately, it's taken for granted and squandered by cynical, self-serving individuals who deride morality and ethics as abstract, foolish principles. Trust comes into play no matter who we are or what we do. It matters very much.

DOING WELL BY DOING GOOD
The importance of generosity can't be overstated

Judging by the news these days you might get the feeling that everyone is out to cheat and steal from everyone else. It might make you wonder what happened to the holiday spirit. Yet I think we still believe that most people are decent, law-abiding citizens trying to make an honest living so they can support themselves and their families. One story a good friend told me recently was certainly reassuring.

The hero was a Chicago cab driver, and it started with my friend's hailing a taxi. The driver was from India and spoke with a heavy accent. A day or so earlier my friend had taken a cab and accidentally left his car keys in the back seat. He told the driver the story about leaving his keys in the other taxi. In fact, my friend thought the cab was from the same company and asked for the firm's phone number. It was then that the driver told a story of his own.

The driver told my friend that a few days earlier he had driven a woman to the Ritz-Carlton Hotel in downtown Chicago. After dropping her off at the hotel, he happened to glance at the back seat while he was at a stoplight and discovered that the woman had left her purse in the cab. The purse contained $2,000 in cash, her passport and a number of credit cards. He immediately returned to the hotel and notified the woman that he had her purse. Naturally she was ecstatic and gave the driver a $200 reward. But there's more. She then asked him for the names of his children so she could send them Christmas presents. She also asked for the address of his cab company so she could send a letter to his bosses praising his honesty. The cab driver, of course, was delighted to supply her with all this information. He ended his story by saying, "If I had taken the $2,000 and spent it on myself, the feeling I got would have lasted only a few hours. But the feeling I got from returning that purse to the lady will last me a lifetime. I will always remember it, and so will my family."

To me those are profound words and so true. There's no better feeling than being able to help other people. It truly is more rewarding to give than to receive. Maybe it's the look in someone's eyes or knowing that you've made someone's heart sing. It just stays with you.

A few years ago there was a story profiling Michael Jordan in one of the Chicago newspapers. In the story he talked about walking down the street one day and being approached by a panhandler. Jordan gave him a $100 bill, and that individual's reaction to Jordan's generosity was obviously one of immense gratitude. But Jordan made the same point as the taxi driver: He got more out of that exchange than the recipient did, because it made him feel like a better person.

Giving can mean a lot of things. It's those little gestures of kindness that help make someone's day. Maybe it's telling colleagues how much they mean to you. Or saying "I love you" to your spouse and children. Some people can't bring themselves to share their love and affection with others, but the importance of hugs, kisses and simple words of love can never be overstated. None of these words or actions cost us a cent, but they can be more valuable to the recipients than a pile of expensive gifts. They come from the heart. They make others feel special and needed, which is what giving is all about. Sometimes we get so wrapped up in ourselves that we don't take the time to look around us. When that happens we miss so much.

Finally, thank you for all your notes, letters and phone calls. They're always welcomed. And may I take this opportunity to wish everyone a most joyous and prosperous New Year. You have given me so much, and it is deeply appreciated. I love you all.

It's all about integrity

A sales icon passes away,
leaving us with his common-sense marketing legacy

Mark McCormack was an individual who had a big impact on my life. I had never heard of him until I came across a book entitled *What They Did Not Teach You At Harvard Business School.* I thought the title was a little unusual and consequently picked up a copy. I couldn't put it down. It was filled with common sense and solid advice—I felt like I had discovered gold.

When I am asked to speak, I often mention the book and what McCormack had to say about dealing with people. That was the genius of Mark McCormack—he knew how to work with others and how to gain their trust and respect by adhering to principles that are in short supply today. He had integrity and the common touch that are so important when talking to and negotiating with others. He was direct, honest and had respect for his clients. He didn't over-promise and he didn't exaggerate. In short, he did business the old-fashioned way. He was honest, and that's why he was so successful. Maybe that's the reason he wrote a sequel to his first book, entitled *What They Still Don't Teach You At Harvard Business School.* McCormack believed in simplicity and doing the right thing. I wish more leaders would take notice of how McCormack not only conducted business but also how focused he was when it came to keeping one's word.

I wasn't the only person who noticed McCormack's talents. *Forbes* listed McCormack as the 209th-richest American, estimating his worth at $1 billion. *Golf* called him "the most powerful man in golf." *Tennis* said he was "the most powerful man in tennis," and *Sports Illustrated* cited him as "the most powerful man in sports." *The Times of London* wrote that he was "one of the 1,000 people who have most influenced the 20th century."

McCormack was owner, chairman and chief executive of IMG, formerly International Management Group, which represented all kinds of sports stars and celebrity talents. His first big-name client was Arnold Palmer, whom he knew from his college days when McCormack played golf for the College of William & Mary and Palmer played for Wake Forest University.

Before signing with McCormack, Palmer had received watches and trophies for winning golf tournaments. McCormack changed all that and, according to an obituary in *The New York Times*, Palmer's annual income went from $50,000 to $500,000 within three years. Eventually, Palmer made $10 million per year.

By 2002, IMG had more than 2,000 employees in 85 offices in 35 nations. IMG negotiated the Tiger Woods' contract with Nike in 2000 for close to $100 million. McCormack obviously loved doing business and enjoyed being in the middle of the action. Just about every major sports star and commentator—from tennis greats Serena and Venus Williams and John McEnroe to quarterback Joe Montana and broadcasters John Madden and Bob Costas—is on the IMG roster. But there are more than just sports stars and commentators. People such as former General Electric Chairman Jack Welch and violinist Itzhak Perlman are part of the group. The list goes on and on.

The reason I mention McCormack is because I believe he probably is one of the greatest salespeople who ever lived.

What stands out most is that McCormack was a salesman's salesman. He approached sports marketing like a consummate salesman. He had the basic instincts and talents of a man who could make things happen. Good salespeople are what I call movers and shakers. They are creative, and when they see an opportunity they go for it. They strategize, work hard and see their clients as often as they can—in person. They may occasionally use e-mail or even voice mail, but what most talented salespeople believe in the most is seeing their customers eyeball to eyeball, and McCormack believed in that formula for success. McCormack's books and advice on how to deal with others are timeless.

McCormack to me represents what integrity is all about. When he made his first deal with Arnold Palmer, they sealed the deal with a handshake. Through his relationship with Palmer, the word obviously got out that you could trust Mark McCormack.

After all, that's what we're all looking for as we journey through life—people we can trust. But trust has to be earned and a relationship takes time and patience. Too many businesses and too many personal relationships go nowhere because trust is absent. I don't believe these are the kinds of things that are taught in business schools around the country. They deal with the latest management fad or what it takes to climb the corporate ladder. Too many academics forget that the things that are important to customers and prospects are honesty, integrity and caring. Look around at the corporate scandals we've endured and witnessed in the past year.

Mark McCormack passed away after having been in a coma since suffering a heart attack. Maybe the legacy he leaves behind is that which he shared in his best-selling books: Stay humble, don't cheat, keep things simple and stay with your core business. They say McCormack was a fierce competitor and hated losing, but that doesn't mean he forgot what ethics and principle are all about. Street smarts are best.

STRONG VALUES AND ETHICS
Both are vital to business success

All of us want to do the right thing. We strive to be good citizens as well as thoughtful and decisive leaders. Whether we're the head of a large corporation or running a department in a small company, we want to excel. If you're like me, you're always looking around to see how other leaders operate. So I'd start with a question: What do Roger Enrico, the dynamic former head of PepsiCo; Andy Grove, who ran Intel; Phil Jackson, head coach of the Los Angeles Lakers; Rear Admiral Ray Smith, a former Navy SEAL; and Jack Welch, former chairman of General Electric, all have in common?

Sure, they're all success-driven. But they share other notable attributes. Enrico, for example, spent much of his time making sure his company was thriving and would flourish in the next century. How? By running a "war college" for a new generation of Pepsi leaders. Grove also believes in the classroom approach. He shared the lessons he has learned in his career with his colleagues and has taught at Stanford University. Welch also believes in mentoring. He regularly participated in the General Electric Leadership Development Institute in New York working with GE executives. Smith, a Vietnam veteran, visits with current SEALs, telling them stories and why it takes courage, honor and teamwork to succeed. And anyone who's followed the Chicago Bulls and Los Angeles Lakers successes knows about Jackson's leadership prowess. He's a skilled teacher and mentor.

What else do these men have in common? First of all, they're what I call idea developers. They all know what it takes to win and do everything they can to help foster a winning culture in their organizations.

They're value promoters. They have strong values that everyone understands and lives up to. The values aren't just stuck on a plaque in the hallway. They're the foundation of the organization, and everybody is held accountable to them.

These men have been energy builders. All the books on management tell you that true leaders seem to have incredible amounts of energy. While the leaders I'm talking about seem to have endless energy, they also energize others. They encourage everyone to stretch their talents and skills.

They're also risk takers. Welch calls it "edge"—the ability to see reality and act on it, make tough decisions, and encourage and reward others who are willing to do the same.

Finally, all are good coaches and storytellers. They are renowned for their abilities to give pep talks, have hallway chats and make terrific speeches. They personalize their vision and ideas by telling stories that hit people in the heart as well as the head.

Gen. Wayne Dowling, former head of U.S. Special Forces, is another individual in the same league. He used to hand out what he called "reinventing licenses" to his people. One side of the card, which was made to look like a driver's license, read: "Is it the right thing for our country? Our forces? Is it consistent with our organization's values? Is it legal and ethical? Is it something you are willing to be held accountable for?" If the answer was yes to all those questions, the advice was simple: "DON'T ASK PERMISSION. JUST DO IT." On the other side of the card, Dowling listed the mission and values of the Special Forces Command: "Prepare Special Operations Forces to successfully conduct worldwide special operations, civil affairs and psychological operations in peace and war...." And then: "WE VALUE: Our people, creativity, competence, courage and integrity."

Two key words here are values and ethics. Show me an organization that doesn't have sound values and ethics, and I'll show you an organization that will eventually fail. Without values and ethics, there is no meaning and there is no plan.

ALWAYS PLAY FAIR
Respect your customers and their chain of command

Sometime ago I was moderator of a fascinating panel discussion during the Federation of American Health Systems' annual conference in Washington. Members of the panel, addressing the purchasing of capital equipment, always a critical issue in healthcare, were a nurse administrator, a chief financial officer and a chief information officer. The panelists each gave 15-minute presentations on how they make capital purchasing decisions at their institutions. Vendors and providers were in the audience, so the session became quite lively. Based on the panelists' remarks and the questions from the audience, there are some trouble spots between vendors and their customers. I'll try to explain.

In my way of thinking, two of the most serious mistakes any selling organization can make are taking customers for granted and going over someone's head in a desperate attempt to save an account. The CFO of one major metropolitan hospital discussed these two sins at length. He talked about a major supplier with a great reputation that wasn't paying attention to the hospital's business. The facility's contract was up for review, and the company had submitted an initial proposal without really doing its homework. Another vendor made a much lower bid, which is when the trouble began. The CFO was candid with the existing vendor, making it clear he was very disappointed with the new bid. The company lowered its bid significantly and even threw in a few extra goodies. But the CFO wasn't sold, and he told the company the contract was in jeopardy.

Now panicked, executives of the vendor did something I believe is totally unprofessional and smacks of bad sales management. They bypassed the CFO—as well as the chief executive officer—and pleaded their case to two members of the board. The move didn't work. The decision was thrown back to the CFO who, needless to say, was furious. He made it clear the vendor's contract would not be renewed.

This isn't an isolated incident. I've heard more and more stories about this type of end-run. I recently participated in two focus groups in which top executives discussed experiences with companies that purposely avoided the purchasing chain of command to get their way. One hospital CIO told of awarding a contract to an information systems vendor after an exhausting review. The supplier that won the business did a very thorough job of meeting the requirements set by the hospital. But an executive of one of the losing vendors became enraged. He sent letters to the hospital's officers, questioning the decision-making process and impugning the integrity of the CIO. Again, the tactic didn't work. The CIO told the group: "I'll never forget what they did."

My advice to all suppliers is simple: First, make sure your employees are staying in touch with your customers on a personal basis. That way you'll head off potential problems early. And when you're asked to make a bid, give it careful consideration and analysis. Don't shoot from the hip. Providers don't want to waste time and play games. They need to know what your best offer is right now, not tomorrow or next week. And if you think someone hasn't given you a fair shot at the business, don't go over that person's head in an attempt to have the decision overruled. Go through channels to make your appeal and accept the decision if it still doesn't go your way. If you fail to do this, remember that people have long memories. A lot more business could be at stake in the future, and you won't have much of a chance.

Everything is fair in love and war, so they say. But of course that's not quite true in the real world. I hear more and more about things like ethics, professionalism and service. Violate any of those and you're gambling with your integrity. I know competition is fierce and sometimes requires a little rule-breaking, but behaving like a spoiled child when things go wrong isn't the way to win business.

PLAYING BY THE RULES PAYS OFF
Ethical behavior usually results in more business

I believe most of us know ethical behavior pays off. It's the only way to go, but from time to time there are stories in the press about companies that cut corners and don't play straight with their employees, customers or shareholders. Many of us might disagree over what exactly constitutes being "ethical," but we know that doing the right thing, keeping your word and not taking advantage of people are part of an ethical business. Of course, some organizations don't believe in doing business this way, but they typically end up failing or paying heavy restitution for their sins. It's an individual's responsibility to live an ethical life, but much of the blame for unethical business behavior starts at the top. Unless the person who runs the outfit instills in colleagues the importance of ethics in everything they do, a dangerous vacuum forms. And that's when the trouble begins.

In an issue of *Business Ethics*, published by Mavis Publications in Minneapolis, there's a story headlined "Does It Pay to be Ethical?" Examples are given of companies that did not conduct themselves ethically and paid dearly for their transgressions. When you hear such stories, it becomes clear why running an organization with a solid ethical foundation is critically important. *Business Ethics* offers some excellent data as evidence to back up the argument.

A Cone/Roper Cause-Related Marketing Trends Report, which is an update of a similar report conducted in 1993, shows that three out of four consumers now use a company's community reputation as a tie-breaker in choosing what to buy and where to shop. In other words, customers obviously support companies that support a few good causes. Home Depot has latched onto this marketing trend by committing itself to community development and youth-at-risk programs. "This is as much a part of our strategy in growing our business as the products we carry and select," says Suzanne Apple of Home Depot. She contends the approach gives the company a "critical competitive advantage."

Avon sponsors an awareness campaign about breast cancer and also pushes the Worldwide Fund for Women's Health. The cosmetics company claims these programs help develop bonds between customers and sales representatives and give customers another reason to buy Avon products.

Walker Research of Indianapolis has found that corporate character is critically important to both customers and investors. Its research shows 75% of consumers refuse to buy from certain companies because of their customer service or business practices. And 26% of those surveyed said social responsibility was extremely important to them in making investment decisions.

A study released in August 1996 by the Center for Corporate Community Relations at Boston College found that employees at two companies, Polaroid and Gillette, believe a company's community involvement is important. They said they feel more loyal to a company that has a strong community presence. Meanwhile, according to research by Vanderbilt University, low-polluting companies, compared with higher-polluting competitors, posted better financial performance in eight out of 10 cases.

Playing by the rules is just good business. Look around you, and the evidence is there. We still admire companies that honor their commitments, care about their communities, treat their employees fairly and don't cheat their customers. That's a pretty good definition of success.

Teed off about cheating
CEOs who lie on the links may be fudging things at the office, too

Every year I play in an amateur golf tournament called Pine to Palm in Detroit Lakes, Minn. For a duffer like me it's a fun time, and my son-in-law, Gerry, plays with me. Neither Gerry nor I would be classified as potential world-beaters because we both shoot in the high 80s or low 90s or worse, but we both love the game. That's because we feel that golf is a personal challenge that requires skill, character and integrity.

Anyone's success on the golf course is dependent on his or her skill, but it's also a test of character and temperament, because this is a tough game. I know that whenever I shoot a better-than-average game, I'm elated because I have been able to control myself and not hurry my shots or become so distracted by anything else so to forget the fundamentals of the game.

Golf is a lot like other sports in that if you haven't played it, it's hard to explain why those of us who do spend so much time chasing a little white ball around the course. Not the least part of the attraction is that golf courses are built in some beautiful spots. The game also brings people together. It's not uncommon to see husbands and wives enjoying time together out on the course. Of course, businesspeople have been getting to know each other while missing two-foot putts forever. As a result, golf is one of the fastest-growing participatory sports in the country, and more courses are being built all the time.

Golf is a game of honor and has been seen as such from its beginnings in Scotland some 600 years ago. There have been many times when a leading golf professional has literally given up the opportunity to win thousands of dollars by voluntarily reporting an incorrect scorecard to tournament officials. Cheating and lying about one's golf score has long been considered a scoundrel's refuge, and anytime I have played with people who fudge on their scores I am disgusted.

That's why I was appalled recently to read an article in *USA Today* about how many top executives admit to cheating at golf.

In a survey commissioned by Starwood Hotels and Resorts, 82% of 401 high-ranking corporate executives admitted to cheating on the links. Much of the article dealt with the possible connection between this type of deceit and the kind of corruption that is played out in the business pages every day right now.

Now I'm sure there are those who would think it's silly to make that kind of connection. Golf's just a game, after all. But I would say they probably haven't played much golf.

Listen to what Jeff Harp, a former banker in Fort Worth, Texas, has to say. He has declined loans to chief executive officers whom he claims to have witnessed cheating at golf. His premise goes like this. Companies borrow for two reasons: either they have an opportunity or they have trouble. As a lender trying to gauge the trustworthiness of a client, he is shocked to see one cheating at golf. Can you blame him?

An organizational psychologist, Ken Siegel, has been interviewing executives for some 25 years and says that most CEOs do not consider themselves liars. As a matter of fact, Siegel says most execs believe their greatest strength is working with people when their subordinates say that it's their greatest weakness. He goes on to say, "(CEOs) lose their ability to distinguish what is honest and what is not. Lies are getting bigger and bigger. We're seeing this played out everywhere now from Tyco to Enron."

Another point of view relating to golf and how CEOs play the game comes from Young Kim-Epstein, a golfer and CEO of Manhattan Wealth Advisors in Los Angeles. She plays golf with men frequently and claims that they have no sense of humor when playing. They throw temper tantrums, bend their clubs and cheat. "If I play better than them, I become really unpopular," she says.

Another executive who was interviewed for the article says his radar goes up when other golfers blame poor shots on the sun or someone coughing. He suggests that execs who behave like this have to be watched.

None other than legendary investor Warren Buffett drew a connection between golf and business before all of the recent business scandals hit. In his 1998 annual letter to Berkshire Hathaway investors, Buffett wrote that nonrecurring write-offs were like reporting four golfing rounds of 80 and one round of 140 rather than actual rounds of 91, 94, 89, 94 and 92. Then in a 2001 letter Buffett used the golf analogy again: "In golf, my score is frequently below par on a pro forma basis. I have firm plans to restructure my putting stroke and therefore only count swings I take before reaching the green."

I can't tell you for sure that there is a correlation between CEOs cheating at golf and cheating in business. But I can tell you that cheating or lying in either venue is unacceptable. After all, a chief executive is supposed to be the moral compass for his or her organization, and when the person at the top is seen cheating, it brings into question the integrity of the whole company.

Maybe some of our CEOs feel they are above the fray and can do what they choose. True leaders, however, are always concerned about how their actions affect those around them and the organizations they lead.

Personally, I simply don't want to be around those who cheat, period, whether it's playing a sport or doing business. You just can't trust them. It all comes down to personal integrity.

TRUST BUST
Greed and illegal actions dominate corporate world,
but we know the solutions

I got into a discussion the other day with my good friend Tony Alibrio about some of the elements of a civilized society that seem to be in short supply these days, such as character, empathy and ethics. Tony knows his stuff, having spent about 37 years as a senior executive in the healthcare industry before retiring in March 2001 as chief of the healthcare division of Sodexho Marriott, where he managed a workforce of 75,000 people and serviced some 1,000 hospitals and long-term care facilities. And he did so with the highest integrity, an example for others to follow.

Tony and I agreed that any successful relationship—be it in one's business or personal life—must involve trust, for which you have to have all three of the elements I just mentioned and more. Trust is an endangered species in our society, from Capitol Hill to the boardroom to the workplace and even to our schools, with disastrous consequences for all.

The reason that Tony and I got on this topic is obvious. Look at what is happening in corporate America. The selfishness, greed and egomania of those involved in some of the most egregious scandals of the past few years have been mind-boggling. The philosophy of those involved—including some in our industry—seems to be self-aggrandizement at all costs.

The pattern keeps repeating. In communications, energy, financial services (mutual funds being the latest), government contracts, medical products and services, sports and just about any other business, you can find people who have forgotten about everything but getting rich. They are willing to flout the laws, endanger their companies and even hurt their own families in the mindless pursuit of dollars they did not earn.

I wonder what happened to these people. I want to know when they lost their moral compass, their sense of duty, their concern for consequences. Did it happen when they were little kids, when they may have been given a sense of entitlement? In college, where they may have skirted the rules and gotten away with it? In their early careers, watching others get paid more handsomely? Maybe the excesses of the "me generation," with its focus on individualism, have come home to roost and we are witnessing the payoff. Whatever it is, these people seem to have had life experiences that taught them that they are not subject to the rules everyone else must follow. They are incapable of contemplating the possibility of disgrace until it's too late.

I know people who roll their eyes when I start talking about trust and ethics, even those in healthcare. But I often wonder how anyone in the business of caring for others cannot understand the need for values. This is a values-based business, after all.

I am absolutely convinced that character, empathy and ethics have to be taught at all levels in schools. We have to teach early and then reinforce the notion that giving in to the temptation to bend or break the rules, even if it seems nobody is watching, is never a good idea—for you or for those around you.

Another part of making our system more ethical is leadership. Great leaders regard themselves as servants to others, not as the font of all wisdom or the only important person in an organization. It is their example that guides an organization, and when the leader lacks strong ethics, that is when things begin to unravel. I submit that one of the reasons for the resurgence of older executives returning to run businesses is because of their value systems. They are bringing back that old-time spirit of the Golden Rule, honesty and integrity.

Perhaps there will be a turnaround in what we have been seeing in our news pages of late, as those who don't feel they should have to abide by the rules of good citizenship and business ethics are weeded out of the leadership posts. Most companies, after all, don't define success as one person getting rich at the expense of everyone else. They view success of the organization as a whole becoming more profitable and productive.

Leadership can only go so far if people aren't willing to be accountable. Those who work in healthcare and other industries have to map out their own mission, values and vision. It helps to have good leaders, but ultimately it is up to everyone in corporate America to honor each other and to work and live honestly.

Tony Alibrio has those values and spent a career inculcating them in others. He has been a super role model for healthcare. In turn, I have always been proud of being involved in healthcare because of the values that 99% of people in the industry bring to taking care of their fellow human beings. Thank you, Tony, for giving me the idea for this column and reminding me what being in business is all about—sharing our common values. It's a privilege.

Chapter **8**

PERSONAL
GROWTH

TREATING PEOPLE WITH RESPECT
It's a practice that's all-too-often ignored

A good friend of mine got a frantic call one Saturday afternoon from a next-door neighbor. The neighbors were having a dinner party that night for some business friends and needed extra help to serve their guests. They had far underestimated the number of people coming and asked if my friend would be willing to help out. He agreed, and that evening he learned a lesson about human behavior.

That night, my friend was struggling to carry a tray of dinners to a certain table. In order to get to the table he had to traverse a very narrow doorway. He called to the people at the table he was serving and asked for some help. He swears the people at the table looked directly at him and then turned their backs. He was aghast but asked for help again. No one lifted a finger. He finally maneuvered his way to the table and served them. But he couldn't get the experience out of his mind. It gave him a better appreciation of how waiters, waitresses and others in service jobs are made to feel when they're treated rudely or ignored altogether. Since my friend is a prominent attorney in Chicago and lives in an upscale suburban neighborhood, it also gave him some insight into the way some of his neighbors view the world. He wasn't impressed.

I'm sure we've all seen this before—people mistreating those they consider to be of lesser station. I really wonder how they justify it to themselves. Is it because they simply don't know how to react, or do they really think they are so much more important than others? I think it has to do with good manners, something too many of us were obviously never taught.

When it comes to how people should be treated, my dad was my role model. He was a salesman all his life. He loved people, and people in turn loved him. No one was ever treated rudely by my father, especially those in what some consider "lowly" service jobs such as waiting tables or collecting garbage. He went out of his way to treat everyone he met with the utmost courtesy because that's what he was taught. And in his travels as a "peddler" in the '30s and '40s he, too, had been on the receiving end of heavy doses of rudeness and rejection. He made it clear to me that treating anyone badly was just about the worst thing you could do. Dad hated phonies and intensely disliked those who had inflated opinions of themselves.

Some of the biggest jerks I've ever met have advanced degrees and fancy job titles. They're very impressed with their own importance and every day find new ways to exhibit arrogance and insensitivity. But individuals who behave this way are usually masking insecurity. Confident people deal with everyone in a friendly and open manner. The world doesn't frighten them, and they take each day as it comes. Notice the leaders you respect the most. What characteristic stands out? I'll bet it's their ability to deal with everyone equally and fairly. And I'll bet they really know how to listen.

If managers would spend more time with their employees, I believe there would be less friction in the workplace. Many top executives are so intent on working on that consolidation plan or negotiating that merger they forget about their own people. Employees are kept in the dark, which is when the rumors start and morale starts to nose-dive. It's a vicious cycle.

My friend, the part-time waiter, got a taste of what so many people have to endure daily just because of ignorance and poor manners. Sometimes life's lessons come at us when we least expect them. When they happen, we should seize the opportunity and learn something. Always reach out.

Start each day with a positive attitude
Cynicism can be harmful to your health

I'm not a fan of cynics. I lump their kind with doom-and-gloomers. They're just no fun to be around. In fact, based on mounting evidence, spending time with them can actually be harmful to one's health. I choose to be with people who are enthusiastic and positive about life and who can't wait to get up in the morning. Don't waste your time with negative people because they'll inevitably drag you down to their level. An upbeat attitude, contagious enthusiasm and a willingness to take on each day as it comes are traits I think most people admire. Such people are the doers. They inspire everyone around them and make a positive contribution every day, not only to themselves but to their organizations and to society.

So it was with interest that I read an article about a session that took place at a convention of the American Psychological Association in Chicago. According to the article in the *Chicago Tribune*, three university professors and two management consultants got together to discuss the topic of cynicism and its psychological impact on Americans' health. But to make the subject more interesting, the group decided to use the comic strip "Dilbert" as part of the discussion. While I'm not a regular reader of the comic strip, I do enjoy it from time to time. Scott Adams, the creator of "Dilbert," portrays the main character as a demoralized computer geek mired in the complexities and isolation of the corporate world. While the "Dilbert" workplace absurdities and his supervisors' foibles can be hilarious, the issues involved have a not-so-funny downside.

The serious side of all this is the fact that a cynical attitude can have a very bad effect on one's health. Research increasingly links cynicism with all kinds of health problems such as cardiovascular disease and immune system dysfunction. Large companies can actually be a health hazard, especially for those without an optimistic outlook on life. Steven Rogelberg, an assistant professor of psychology at Bowling Green State University in

Ohio, made some interesting observations during the panel discussion in Chicago. "Maybe corporate cynicism has something to
do with data showing that CEOs earn 85 times more money on
average than the average employee," he says. "Another problem is
the emergence of the team approach. It busts up the way things
are done and creates lots of uncertainty."

Meanwhile, the results of a study of some 7,300 British civil
servants, published in the respected medical journal *Lancet*, show
that people who had little or no control over their jobs had a 16
times higher risk of a heart attack than their bosses.

According to the *Tribune* article, Bruno Cortis, M.D., a cardiologist in River Forest, Ill., claims cynicism also is part of the
newly identified Type-H personality—found in hostile, aggressive
individuals—which appears to lead to cardiovascular problems,
including heart attacks. These people apparently are even more
susceptible to such deadly maladies than the classic type-A, high-
strung person. "Cynicism disconnects you from other people,"
Cortis adds.

There's obviously more to the subject of cynicism, but at the
very least it isn't hard to figure out that a bad attitude can have
some very serious health consequences. Being optimistic is the
only way to approach life in this complicated world. In my opinion, cynics are dream-busters. They only make life more difficult
by always emphasizing the negative. They can never see the silver
lining. That's unfortunate, and it's a prescription for failure.

Life is full of opportunity if one has the right attitude. And
the right attitude is a healthy attitude. The glass is half full.

ATTITUDE IS EVERYTHING
Despite his situation, Robert Horn remains an optimist

As I write this letter, it's really hot in Chicago. According to the weather page in one of the local newspapers, it's hotter here than in Atlanta, Houston and a lot of other places known for their sultry summer weather. Everybody is complaining about the heat and humidity. But if you're alive and healthy, isn't it wonderful that you can experience another day in peace and freedom, no matter how temporarily uncomfortable it might be? Somehow we lose our perspective about how tough things really are in some people's lives.

I just finished reading a book titled *How Will They Know If I'm Dead?* by Robert C. Horn III. Horn is professor emeritus of political science at California State University in Northridge. He and his wife, Judy, have three grown children. For many years, Horn and his family have been very active in soccer circles, and he was instrumental in bringing girls' soccer to the Los Angeles school system. But in June 1988, Bob Horn was diagnosed with amyotrophic lateral sclerosis, or ALS, more commonly known as Lou Gehrig's disease. The disease is a particularly insidious one. In a short time, the muscles atrophy to the point of total paralysis, and in the end the individual usually suffocates to death, usually within two to four years after diagnosis. While the disease takes its brutal toll on the body, the mind is unaffected, so the patient is well aware of the relentless physical deterioration taking place.

But Horn has defied the odds. He wrote his book while almost totally paralyzed, using a word processor with a special hook-up that allows him to tap out his messages with his right foot. I learned these details from a friend of mine, Mike Leonard, who does vignette-type pieces for NBC's "Today" show. His piece on Horn appeared recently, and to say it was powerful and inspirational is an understatement. There's so much Horn can teach us about life. Talk about a positive attitude! Horn epitomizes the eternal optimist. Defeat and self-pity are nowhere to be found.

Here's an excerpt from Horn's book that gives a glimpse of how he looks at life: "I have found along with many others, that despite the difficult conditions of disability and terminal illness, life can be meaningful, productive, fulfilling, rewarding and valuable. I believe that the things I can do are more important than those I can't. There is much more to life than physical ability. I am still a vibrant, healthy and independent person mentally, emotionally and spiritually. I can think, reason, analyze, remember, read, write, learn and communicate. I can love, feel happiness and sadness, be enthusiastic, get angry, have highs and lows, feel joy. I can believe, hope and have faith." Horn's message is one of hope, not despair.

His secret must be his attitude. Something that has had a lasting impact on him is a passage by Charles Swindoll that Horn quotes in his book. Swindoll wrote: "The longer I live, the more I realize the impact of attitude on life. To me attitude is more important than facts. It is more important than the past, than education, than money, than circumstances, than failures, than successes, than what other people think or say or do. It is more important than appearance, giftedness or skill. It will make or break a company, a church, a home. The remarkable thing is we have a choice every day regarding the attitude we will embrace for that day. We cannot change our past. We cannot change the fact that people will act in a certain way. We cannot change the inevitable. The only thing we can do is play the one string we have, and that is our attitude ... I am convinced that life is 10% what happens to me and 90% how I react to it."

Get a big dose of positive thinking and the right attitude and read Horn's book. It just might change your life. Better still, you'll realize how lucky you are.

Caring, believing, doing

Having the right attitude is the key to true success in business and in life

The older I get the more I realize the importance of attitude. I see so many people who have all the attributes that make for success, but for some reason they don't seem to be able to get there. I've witnessed other people with mediocre skills who excel through hard work and sacrifice, propelled by a can-do spirit.

People with positive outlooks see the world as filled with opportunity and the potential of adventure. That's what life really is: an adventurous journey. When we start our trek, none of us really knows how the whole thing is going to turn out. Some have a harder time than others. They're marked right off the bat with hardship, such as the loss of a parent, poverty, poor education and worse. But some who have had a rough start still manage to succeed, perhaps driven by their bad experiences to get somewhere better.

Maybe that is the problem with people who are handed success on a silver platter. They have gone to the right schools, met all the right people, and there is a sense of entitlement that they will get everything they need and want. But what happens is they lack the drive, the empathy for others around them and everything else you need to really succeed in life. They are unprepared for the kind of adversity others know all too well.

I've met others who have the equivalent of an eighth-grade education who have been famously successful because they love life, work hard, know how to deal with people and always have a positive attitude. I've noticed that these individuals usually have the greatest appreciation for their country and everything for which it stands.

Another part of success is humility, a trait lacking in many who have been handed things. Many of these people cannot bring themselves to accept honest and straightforward advice. They feel they are being personally insulted when someone critiques their efforts. Conversely, most top achievers I've met in my career have humility about themselves that makes others want to help them in whatever project they undertake. They also have no qualms about asking for help. They don't pretend to know something when they don't. They'll tell you right off the bat, "I don't know."

Those who achieve things got that way by meeting adversity head-on. Too many people today who have gone to the so-called right schools and enjoyed lifestyles others lack sometimes don't have the heart or stamina to stick things out when the going gets tough. Those of us who have had to strive to get to where we are have learned to pick ourselves up from a hit and get back on the field of play. Of course, there are critics who think this kind of blind courage is all senseless and a little too blue-collar, but frankly this kind of attitude is what I look for in my friends and colleagues.

In my opinion, being the most enthusiastic and positive person you know can be a ticket to success. There are doom-and-gloomers all over the place, playing armchair generals. They love to drag others down to their level, which is one of unhappiness and self-loathing. They are what I call losers. Sometimes they come wrapped in attractive packages, but once the action starts their real colors show. They usually run for the sidelines and become spectators instead of getting on the field of play and helping their teammates. They take the easy way out and spend most of their time grousing about how unfair life is and always feel sorry for themselves. They love to take and not give, and, like any disease, they can bring others down with their negative attitudes. Get away from such people. They will take your dreams away.

Finally, for one or two of my friends who are going through some tough times I would like to leave these thoughts with you, by an unknown author:

"If you think you are beaten, you are. If you think you dare not, you don't. If you like to win, but think you can't, it's almost a cinch you won't. If you think you will lose, you are lost. For out in the world we find success begins with a fellow's will; it's all in the state of mind. For many a race is lost ere even a step is run, and many a coward fails ere even his work is begun. Think big and your deed will grow, think small and you will fall behind. Think that you can and you will—it's all in the state of mind. If you think you are outclassed, you are. You have got to think high to rise. You have got to be sure of yourself before you win a prize. Life's battles don't always go to the stronger or faster man. But sooner or later, the man who wins is the man who thinks he can." Attitude is the key.

Opening up to others
Take time for personal communication

On a recent plane trip to the West Coast I had a most interesting experience with a senior executive of a major consulting firm. When I first found my seat it was obvious this fellow really wasn't in the mood for idle chatter. He was on his cell phone talking to some colleagues about a project they were working on, and he seemed less than jovial. So I kept my mouth shut and read the newspapers I had brought with me. Then everyone was told to turn off their cell phones, laptops and other electrical appliances until the flight was airborne. My seatmate complied with the flight attendant's request, and off we went.

There still wasn't too much conversation between us because I wanted to read the papers, and he apparently wanted to think. That was the situation until we had been airborne about 10 minutes. I watched him remove his briefcase from under the seat in front. As he opened the case he let out some four-letter words. Obviously he was missing something, and was very unhappy about it.

I asked him if I could help and he blurted out, "I just bought a brand-new laptop and had it all programmed and left it at the security checkpoint at O'Hare. I don't know what to do. I only had the thing for two days. How stupid can one person be?"

And so began a series of phone calls to his Chicago office, where his administrative assistant said she would go out to O'Hare and see if she could locate the computer at lost and found. The flight attendant in first class also offered her help by giving my seatmate a phone number he could call at O'Hare.

The poor fellow was literally beside himself but after a time began to settle down, and we began to talk.

He told me about his family. We talked about his job and he told me how much he missed his wife and kids as he traveled around the country and the world. We talked about business, about how competitive things have become.

I sensed a certain melancholy in him as we talked. His dream was to retire early and get out of the "rat race." You could tell he cared about his career and his family, and I'm sure from our conversation he has a hard time balancing the two just as a lot of us do. We also talked about topics like religion, politics and the war in Afghanistan. We really got to know each other, and the conversation was both enlightening and fun.

Then he told me something I'll always remember: "You know something, Chuck, I never talk about the things you and I have discussed with anyone. I simply don't have the time. I'm worried about recovering my laptop, but maybe I should leave it at home more. This has been great for me and I hope you have enjoyed it as well."

Funny how wrapped up we get in our work at the expense of our personal growth and understanding. I see it happen all the time. Men and women who give so much to their work that they sacrifice the ones they should care most about: their families. That's not preaching; that's a fact. They also sacrifice their feelings and emotions by not getting them out in the open so they can examine them and get a fix on where their lives are headed.

I've run into any number of successful individuals who have done incredible things in their careers but whose personal lives are a mess. They simply don't take the time to find out what's really important. How empty they must feel at times. It just seems we are in so much of a hurry these days that we too often forget some of the simple things that make everyday living an adventure.

One, of course, is talking with others, and another is reaching out to others for advice and help.

I believe many businesses lack direction because they have not taken the time to work out their mission, vision and values as an organization. The same examination should take place in the lives of the people who run those organizations. I submit that too often individuals who do not have personal goals and expectations are rudderless and consequently less focused and productive. And that can lead to careers that falter and die.

Part of this self-examination is having the courage to talk to others around you, and not just family members. Use your colleagues as sounding boards about where you are going within the organization, just as you would use them to discuss where the organization is going. Talk to people outside, even if they are just strangers on a plane. And maybe leave the cell phones and laptops back at the office.

Competent leaders will have a pretty good grip on the priorities of their organizations. But this doesn't take place in a vacuum. They need the advice and opinions of others to bring things into focus. Listening to and getting to know others is a critical element in the tricky business of leading.

ENTHUSIASM IS INFECTIOUS
A positive attitude goes a long way

Why is it that people have a difficult time being honest about what they love? We're living in an age when most individuals are embarrassed to admit that they're passionate about their jobs. In many cases it opens them to ridicule from their colleagues. People just aren't supposed to like their work. If they do, psychologists might say their priorities are out of whack or they don't have their lives in proper balance. But excellence is achieved only if a person finds some enjoyment in the workplace. The type of job doesn't matter. What some might see as drudgery others might find challenging and fulfilling—and they show it. Their enthusiasm becomes contagious, lifting everyone's spirits.

There's no secret to enthusiasm. It's an attitude that anyone can develop, but it takes discipline and courage. Starting out the morning saying "I'm going to give today 100%" is a good way to get fired up. Waking up early also helps get a head start on the day. One of the great adages of all time is that the early bird truly does catch the worm. Getting to a meeting before others arrive gives you time to think and to prepare. And even to relax. Again, anybody can do this, but a lot of people just loathe the idea of getting up early. Consequently they miss opportunity after opportunity.

Enthusiasm and passion also come more easily when you're feeling good about yourself and the world around you. It helps to put a smile on your face. Sometimes it almost hurts to smile. You have a headache, you've had a fight with your mate, or the weather is gloomy. They're all good excuses for wearing a frown. But try a smile anyway. Give everyone you encounter a smile. Couple that with a cheerful "hello" and the magic begins. People are attracted to others who have a positive outlook on life. None of us likes to be around doom-and-gloomers. We like to feel good, and someone approaching us with a smile and a pleasant greeting usually makes us feel better. Manners come into play as well. Hold the door open for someone. Give up your seat on a bus or train. People crave to be treated with dignity and respect. And you'll feel so good about yourself.

Over the years I've watched certain individuals achieve success even though they didn't necessarily have the natural talent others possessed. What they did have was the ability to work hard and persevere. And they certainly had enthusiasm. Sometimes those who have talent don't think they have to try as hard as others. They take too much for granted and consequently don't give their best effort. That's the biggest reason individuals fail. They don't pay attention to detail, assuming that others will pick up the slack. Achievers and winners are gluttons for detail. They go the extra mile to do everything necessary to attain a certain goal. They love accountability and always take on more than their share when participating in any project. They don't pout and feel burdened.

We all want to be recognized and appreciated. We want to make our mark and be part of something meaningful. The easiest way I know to achieve those goals is to make things happen by your energy and enthusiasm. Have you ever heard of anyone being condemned for working too hard? I haven't. Have you ever heard of anyone being criticized for being too enthusiastic? I hope not. It's always refreshing to see someone with a can-do attitude. Success is really up to you. Hard work does pay off. It will never go out of style.

ALL IN A DAY'S WORK
A heartwarming story of thoughtfulness

Watch the TV news or read the newspaper and you might begin to think the world is going downhill fast. More shootings. More gang violence. More war. Another day, another corruption arrest or fraud indictment. Nothing seems to be on the square. The picture is not very pretty. But every once in a while along comes a story that partially restores your faith in mankind. In Chicago, for instance, it could be about the fellow who discovered a woman's purse on a seat after a Cubs' baseball game and returned it to the woman with everything in order. Or there's the story of the cabbie in New York City who spent an inordinate amount of time helping a non-English-speaking immigrant locate some relatives in Brooklyn. Yes, there are good people all over this great country of ours who are decent, honest and law-abiding. They care about others and daily make sacrifices to help those in need. But that isn't necessarily the type of story that makes headlines. Because of that we miss out on truly inspiring stories. I recently came across one that I'd like to share.

I found this story in a publication called *Waste News*, which is owned by the same company that publishes *Modern Healthcare*. *Waste News* covers the news in waste management from product design to disposal and recovery. Unless you're in the industry or interested in such issues, a lot of what you read in the publication might be pretty esoteric stuff. But one story on the front page sure caught my attention. Headlined "Band of Gold," it tells the story of two city recycling workers in Roanoke, Va., who returned some wedding rings to a very relieved 80-year-old woman, who has been married for some 60 years.

According to the story in *Waste News*, the incident started innocently enough. Dot Seigler's morning ritual sounds fairly typical. She reads the morning paper, does the Jumble puzzle and has a cup of coffee. However, this particular morning as she was doing the puzzle, she looked down at her hand and noticed her rings were gone. She checked her jewelry box, but they weren't there.

Then she called her sister to search the sofa where she sat during a visit the day before. She even looked on her driveway and in the front yard. As she was checking the front yard she noticed a recycling truck starting to come up the hill but didn't pay much attention because she was starting to worry about the whereabouts of her rings. However, a few moments after she went back into the house, there was a knock at the front door. Seigler opened the door to find one of the city recycling workers standing there. "Lady, did you lose something?" he asked her. He then opened his hand, and there were two of her rings. Ricardo Rogers and co-worker Ronnie Laughlin had noticed Seigler searching her front yard as they drove by. When Laughlin dumped her recycled paper into his truck, out popped the rings.

Seigler described what had happened: "Normally I wear my rings on my ring finger." But because her arthritis had flared up she had switched the rings to another finger. "The rings were quite tight on my little finger." But by the time Seigler had finished stuffing old newspapers into a plastic bag for recycling day, the swelling had subsided, which is when the rings fell off. With two rings recovered, Seigler and the two men then found the third missing ring in the plastic bag that had contained the newspapers. Seigler's 87-year-old husband was also relieved when the rings were found: "I was astonished. We looked in all the normal places. It was a real surprise, and we're real happy."

Laughlin and Rogers didn't think they had done anything special. "She lost them. We found them. It's just our job to return them to her," Laughlin said. The Seiglers have rewarded the two men, and so has the Roanoke City Council.

It's just a simple story about honesty. All in a day's work, the two men would tell you. Nothing too scintillating. But it sure is nice to read about the good guys once in a while. They made a difference.

GOING THE DISTANCE
The power of motivation

I recently received a new computer as a gift. A few days ago as I was trying to make room for this new technology in my study at home, I came across a couple of books that brought back some bittersweet memories. Both were written by the late George Sheehan, M.D., one of my heroes. In his last book, *Going the Distance*, he talks about his life and his fight against cancer. He lost his battle in November 1993 at the age of 74. I remember being so pained by his death that I found it difficult to deal with for some time.

Over many years he had given me so much inspiration, especially in the early years of *Modern Healthcare* when things weren't quite as rosy as they are today. Oftentimes when I felt down I would pick up one of his books, and his words would always renew my spirit. Sheehan was the oldest of 14 children. He was a cardiologist and record-setting runner.

My first encounter with his wisdom came in 1972 when I read one of his columns in *Runner's World* magazine. From then on I was an avid fan. He wrote seven books, including *Running and Being*, *Personal Best* and *This Running Life*. His writings and views on life are brilliant, and his books are a wonderful legacy, continuing to challenge all of us to live passionately.

He believed that all of us have within us the ability to not only pursue excellence but to achieve it. He used words like will, commitment and passion in all his writings. He also believed some of the biggest heroes in life were those who got on the field of play and lost but never gave up.

In his book *Personal Best*, in a chapter titled "The Many Levels of Motivation," he talks about the critical importance of desire. "Motivation is the need, drive, or desire to act in a certain way to achieve a certain end," he writes. "Basic needs are strong motivators. When I am hungry or thirsty or cold, or when I am in obvious danger, I am impelled to do something about it. I am willing to attack the problem head-on: I do what must be done.

Whereas drives push, desires pull. I have desires for many things. I want self-esteem. I would like to be a hero. I wish to have peak experiences. I pray for the perfect communion with another person. And as I sit here at the typewriter I am trying to write a perfect essay.

"Making allowances for differences in vocation and avocation, I presume you would say much the same. Our needs, drives, and desires—the stuff of our lives—do not vary to any great degree. Yet our motivation does. I see about me people who, in philosopher William James' expression, lead lives inferior to themselves. And I suspect that I do the same. We could all be artists and athletes and heroes. We could all care for orphans and widows and visit the sick. We could all be catchers in the rye, each in his or her own unique and particular way announcing the Creator's intentions at our births. We could be our best. But we are not."

That's powerful stuff. But there's much more to contemplate in his writings. Later in the same chapter he adds: "The Declaration of Independence states unequivocally that all men are created equal. Yet every day I find reason to believe this to be untrue. I run in a race and half the field beats me. I attend a seminar and can't follow the reasoning of the speaker. I read a book and I am unable to understand what is evident to others. Daily I am instructed in my deficiencies. I do something, physical or mental, and realize how far I fall short of what other people accomplish. But I am more than a mind-body complex. I am a soul as well. I share with everyone on this planet one power infinitely more important than talent: willpower. In this power of the soul, all of us are created equal."

In other words, the ability to sacrifice, to go the distance and to be the best no matter what the odds, is in all of us. However, too many turn away because they just don't have the stamina or the intestinal fortitude. Or they just can't bear the risk of failure. Willpower is in all of us if we only choose to employ it.

OVERCOMING OBSTACLES
Achievers get on with their lives

Everybody seems to love being near legendary golfer Arnold Palmer. Even today, on the senior golfers' tournament circuit, he's still a big draw. "Arnie's Army" of fans consider him, among other things, a good father and husband and a regular fellow who has never let fame go to his head. Consequently, a number of people have looked for all kinds of explanations for Palmer's great competitive spirit and success. A significant clue might be a plaque that is said to hang on his office wall; it reads:

If you think you are beaten, you are.
If you think you dare not, you don't.
If you like to win, but think you can't,
It's almost certain you won't.

Life's battles don't always go
To the stronger woman or man,
But sooner or later, those who win
Are those who think they can.

That philosophy should be on every salesperson's wall. It's what living is all about. Taking risks, having confidence in yourself, always going for the gold ring and living passionately. In short, each day counts, and having a negative attitude does nothing for anyone.

And then I read a story about a fellow in Indianapolis, by the name of Darrell Colson, who is confined to a wheelchair. Four years ago Colson, a former tree trimmer, was paralyzed from the waist down after falling from a tree. A tough break for anyone, but Colson hasn't given up. As a matter of fact, just a few weeks ago he saved the life of 20-year-old Orain Williams, who almost drowned.

He was leaving an apartment complex with his fiancé, who noticed a woman lying at the bottom of the pool. The 34-year-old Colson, who swims for therapy, immediately rolled his wheelchair to the edge of the pool and dived in. Williams was submerged in about eight feet of water, but Colson was able to drag her to the edge of the pool. His fiancé helped him lift her out and performed cardiopulmonary resuscitation until help arrived. Colson, by the way, is unemployed and has a son who regularly visits the pool. Over the past few months, he has practiced getting into the pool quickly so he could get to his son if anything happened.

That story should inspire all of us. Why is it so many individuals with so-called handicaps are able to perform such incredible feats? Stories similar to this one appear in newspapers every week. Maybe people who endure physical mishaps have a better perspective of what life is all about. They don't wallow in self-pity and sob stories; they simply get on with their lives and do incredible things—like saving other people's lives. Maybe they realize what Palmer discovered decades ago: If you think you can, you will.

Don't let others set your agenda
You are in control of your destiny

How many of us have had somebody tell us along the way we couldn't do something because we just didn't have what it takes? Maybe it was talent, size, looks or intelligence that we supposedly lacked. I'll bet many of us have been given some of this advice at one point or another. And maybe some of us have succumbed, allowing others to change our direction in life. That's a tragedy. Never let anyone else take your dreams away. If you truly believe in yourself and want something badly enough to make sacrifices and discipline yourself to press on, then I predict you'll make it. But the secret is knowing what you want and how hard you're willing to work for it.

Many years ago I was a candidate for a great job with a leading business publication. The top sales executive knew me personally and said he wanted me on his team. I was in my mid-20s after having served in the Army during the Korean War and then doing some graduate work at Northwestern University's Medill School of Journalism. The publication had a policy of giving each job candidate an aptitude test. I remember taking it and answering all the questions as honestly as I could. One of the questions was: Would you cross the street to get to the other side to avoid a person you knew and didn't like? My answer was yes. Later I was told I had flunked the test because I was too introverted. That very question was used by the person who graded the test to tell me I should explore other career choices. I couldn't believe what I was told. I have always loved people and considered myself quite outgoing. I knew I would do well in sales.

The fellow who had sponsored me as a leading sales candidate was so upset he arranged for me to take another sales test. I passed it with flying colors, and since that time selling has been my profession. When I advise people to never let others make determinations for them or discourage them from doing something they truly desire, I know what I'm talking about. There's really no way to measure what is in a person's heart.

This reminds me of a story I heard a long time ago, involving Fred Astaire's first screen test. He did it all. He sang and danced up a storm, but midway through his test the person in charge interrupted Astaire's routine and said something like: "Mr. Astaire, thank you for coming. However, I suggest you look at the possibility of another line of work. I don't mean to discourage you, but you don't dance very well and you certainly can't sing. Good day, sir." That was it. Just like that somebody had tried to take Astaire's dreams away. Of course Astaire didn't buy it and went ahead and practiced even harder, eventually becoming an entertainment legend. Years later a reporter asked him to explain his success. He answered: "For a fellow who can't dance very well and certainly can't sing, I have been very lucky. People have been good to me."

In an issue of *Speechwriter's Newsletter* comes yet another example of why we should never cave in when someone tells us we're just not cut out to do something: Nancy Stokes Milnes, wife of world-famous baritone Sherrill Milnes, relayed a story in *The New York Opera Newsletter*, which might inspire all of us when we feel like giving up:

"Once, Sherrill and I were having dinner with a very well-known coach. We played a recording of Sherrill in college and asked the coach, 'What do you think about this voice?' And he said, 'Oh, there's not a chance. Don't encourage this person. Tell him to get a day job.' When we told him that the singer was Sherrill, that coach said, 'You know, I'll never discourage another singer again.' "

Rely on your instincts and never give up on yourself. Make your dreams come true! It's your life.

Chapter 9

FROM
THE
HEART

A LETTER FROM THE HEART
Some advice for a lifetime,
from a grandfather who has been waiting for this

To my new granddaughter, Diane Dorothy, I say welcome to the world. Welcome into the Van Treeck and Lauer families. Kathleen and Gerry—your mom and dad—have wanted you for the longest time and now, suddenly, you're here. All 5 pounds, 10 ounces of you. None of us can get over how beautiful, cute, precious and darling you are. I've heard you described over and over that way by family members, friends, well wishers and complete strangers. Everybody believes you are very special, including me, who loves you very, very much.

Being your new grandfather I would like to give you some advice and comments about your future—it will be a rich future because you have a mother and father who are completely devoted to you.

After all, your parents went through an awful lot to bring you into their lives. The adoption process in this country is tough, with the adoptive couple's finances being checked, plus their legal backgrounds and personal histories. Lawyers are hired and all kinds of laws are involved. The paperwork is onerous. And none of that prepares you for waiting for a child. In the case of your parents, Diane, they waited for five long years to find you. There were a lot of dreams and disappointments along the way. But they persevered and didn't let their dreams be taken away, and then they found out about you.

Now that you've arrived, you can see and feel the fulfillment in their lives. Your mom, Kathy, is a giving person. She has a heart that is so large and so willing to give to others that I often fear she will be hurt because of her openness and sensitivity. But she's managed to survive 38 years of living and now has you. You've made your mother a complete person, so you've already made your mark in this world.

Then, there's Gerry, your father. There's not a more loyal, principled, moral person alive. Gerry is one in a million. He is a

250-pound giant who has always loved contact sports and yet is one of the gentlest men I have ever known. He is so special and even though he beats me at golf too often, I consider him a dear, dear friend. So you've got two wonderful parents who love you very much and that is so important. Love, you see, true love is really very special, and as you get older and possibly have your own children, you'll see how wonderful true love can be. But you have come to your mom and dad at a very wonderful time and you have been born free in this great nation where you can pursue your dreams and be just about anything you want to be: a physician, an airline pilot, an investment banker, a nurse or teacher.

The possibilities are endless. Nowadays, every avenue is open to women, so don't be afraid to dream and then make your dreams come true. Give 110% every day and be involved in just about everything you can. Be the most enthusiastic and positive person you can be and don't let others determine your moods. It's your life, your career and your dreams, and nobody owns you. Your most rigid and exacting critic will be yourself, so set your standards high. Don't strive for mediocrity, strive to be the best. Too many individuals go through life letting things happen to them. They enjoy being bystanders and don't get on the field of play. But that's where the action is, where you'll have incredible experiences, some good, some bad. You'll meet some amazingly wonderful people. Furthermore, don't be afraid to ask for help along the way. People basically enjoy helping others and I hope you will, too, as others come to you for guidance and assistance.

There are so many other things, of course, and one of them is honesty and integrity. Be truthful and forthright in everything you do. Cheaters and liars are really losers and cynics. They demean others and bring them down to their level of lost dreams and cheapness. Don't get near people of this ilk, and if they come near you, get away from them as fast as you can.

On the other hand, don't be afraid to emulate and copy those who demonstrate qualities of honesty, loyalty and integrity. Those basic traits are still the qualities that make all the difference in the world and are so admired by everybody. Your integrity is the most important thing you have and never, but never, let anyone take it away from you.

Be loyal. Loyal to your friends, loyal to your parents, loyal to your colleagues and, most important, loyal to yourself, that's what really counts. Don't let yourself down. You will be your own worst critic and that's as it should be, but don't be too hard on yourself. Give yourself some space once in a while so you can look around from time to time and enjoy the world. Also enjoy who you are and what you stand for and what you believe in, and don't waver or give up your ideals because that is what makes you special and so wonderful.

There's something else I want to touch on. Don't be afraid to love and cherish this great nation we live in and the bountiful blessings that have been bestowed upon us. Freedom of religion comes to mind as well as the freedom to be any person you want to be. Be thankful you were born in the United States of America and be thankful that you are now part of a family that will love you forever no matter what happens.

You've already made your mom and dad happy by just being who you are: a healthy, happy baby full of energy. It's as simple as that, and I've discovered over the years that sometimes the simplest things are often the most profound.

That's about it, Diane. I'll be here if you need me, as will your parents. You've got a wonderful life ahead of you, full of promise, adventure and opportunity. I'm confident you will do well. Good luck, sweetheart.

LETTER TO A NEW GRANDSON
Welcome to the world, Patrick John

Welcome Patrick John Lauer, all 7 pounds and 5 ounces of you. You're my sixth grandchild, and according to your parents, you're probably the last. At least that's what they're telling me now.

Patrick, your family is so happy that you've joined us—and there are a lot of us. We all love you so much. There's Dad, Randy, who is my son—and Mom, Wendi, as well as your brothers, Chuck, Ted, Matt and Jack, and your sister, Emma. They couldn't wait for you to join all the fun. And don't forget your grandma and grandpa.

I thought you might like a little help with who's who and what's what in your family. First of all, your mom and dad are incredible. They are both totally dedicated to you and your brothers and sister. They always wanted a large family and now they have one. They are literally surrounded by love. Both your mom and dad are high achievers. I have no doubt where your siblings get all their energy. Your brothers and sister truly are balls of fire. They just keep going and going, and I have a feeling it won't be long before I'll be saying the same thing about you. The nicest thing of all, something I'm sure you'll notice soon enough, is that your mom and dad are very much in love with each other, even more so now than at their wedding nine years ago.

I envy you, Patrick. You have so much to look forward to. First of all, you have been born a citizen of the United States of America. You're a free person, Patrick. You can do anything and be anything. You'll have so many choices. But you'll have to work hard, and it will take some time before everything falls into place. So much is happening today, and so much more awaits you in the years ahead. Don't be afraid to get out on the playing field and take a few chances.

Be open to counsel from family and friends. Most important, listen to your mom and dad. They are the real thing, and they will love you unconditionally forever. Take advantage of their wisdom and experience. And remember you'll only have one mom and dad in your lifetime, so love them and respect them. Respect others too, regardless of race, color or creed.

As much as possible, try to find humor in life. Laugh and smile, and do both as much as you can and with great gusto. You should smile not just because it makes you feel good but because it makes others feel good as well. Laughing is as American as apple pie, and it relieves tension and helps put you in a positive frame of mind about everything. The adage is true: Laughter really is the best medicine.

Finally, Patrick, always have a positive attitude. Be thankful you're alive, be thankful you're living in the USA and be thankful for peace, love and good health. Your attitude will determine your destiny in life. Work hard to be upbeat, give 100% of your being to everything you do and try to always be a decent person. Nobody can ask you for much more than that.

Love, grandpa,

Charles S. Lauer

THE TRIP OF A LIFETIME
Driving his pregnant daughter to the hospital

You read about something like this in the newspapers and think it could never happen to you. Until it does. The day started off routinely enough. I walked my dog first thing in the morning, fed him and started upstairs to get ready for work. Then the phone rang and I heard the question: "Dad, what are you doing?" It was my son calling from his office in downtown Chicago.

"I'm getting ready for work. Why?"

His reply: "Well, it looks like Wendi is ready to deliver and I need someone to bring her downtown to the hospital." Wendi is my daughter-in-law who was pregnant with their fourth child. I hustled over to pick her up a few minutes away in the suburbs for the ride to downtown Chicago. When I arrived, she certainly looked ready to deliver and was experiencing some discomfort. So off we went. To say I was nervous would be the understatement of the year.

As we backed out of the driveway I made the decision to take an alternate route I felt would be faster. It was the height of the rush hour, and I knew it would take us close to an hour to make it to the hospital. Wendi had given birth to her three sons at Northwestern Memorial Hospital in Chicago, which is where she was determined to have her fourth child. I have taken the route I chose that morning many times. Occasionally there are slow-downs, but traffic usually moves right along. I prayed that would be the case that morning. I kept assuring Wendi that I knew what I was doing and that things would work out just fine.

For the first half of the trip everything went smoothly. I was quite proud of myself for my decision-making prowess under fire. But then disaster struck. Traffic started to move at a snail's pace. I was beside myself while trying to reassure Wendi the traffic would let up soon. But it really never did. It was stop-and-go all the way. Wendi became more and more uncomfortable and I began to feel guilty for having chosen that route. Things became even worse when Wendi told me I should start going through red lights and that I always seemed to be in the lane that wasn't moving. She was quite explicit about my navigational skills. I kept my cool, and we were slowly getting closer to the hospital. By this time Wendi was moaning and I felt as though I had just run a marathon.

Traffic came to a halt again about 200 yards away from the hospital, which is when I lost it. I noticed a policeman was directing traffic and for some reason was only holding up the lane we were in. I couldn't stand it any longer. I jumped out of the car and yelled at the policeman: "I've got a woman in this car who's ready to deliver. Get this traffic moving!" The cop looked at me and retorted, "If that's the case get her to a hospital!" My comeback was something like: "That's what I'm trying to do if you would get some of this traffic out of the way!" He did, and moments later we pulled up to the hospital entrance where my son was waiting. He carried Wendi out of the car and put her into a wheelchair. As I drove off to park a couple of blocks away, I felt like someone had hit me with a sledgehammer.

Now the best part. Six minutes after I dropped Wendi off she delivered a healthy, beautiful baby girl weighing 6 pounds and 8 ounces. Her name is Emma Katherine Lauer. What a miracle, and what a dream. Finally, a granddaughter. Will she be spoiled? Of course she will. Will she be Grandpa's girl? Of course. And will my wife and I love her forever just like we do the boys— Teddy, Charlie and Matt? You bet we will! Those are all sure things. And there's one other sure thing: I'm not Mario Andretti, by any means.

To his new granddaughter
Live every day to the fullest

Recently I shared the story about my rather tense ride to the hospital with my daughter-in-law, who six minutes after we arrived gave birth to a healthy 6-pound, 8-ounce baby girl. My son, Randy, and his wife, Wendi, already have three wonderful boys, Chuck, Ted and Matt. This time around they were hoping for a girl, and their dreams came true. What a blessing, and what a thrill. Every time I see a baby, I think about what a miracle it is. It's beyond comparison. To Emma Katherine Lauer, welcome to the world. I watched the reaction of your brothers when you first came home, and they think you are very special. We all do, which is why I wanted to share some thoughts about your future.

First of all, I love you, straight and simple. I promise I'll be around as long as I can to support you in whatever you choose to do with your life. What a future you have. Don't waste a moment of it. Too many people become spectators in life, fearing to get onto the field of play because they might lose. But that's not what life is all about. Life is about reaching for the stars. It's an adventure that's filled with mystery, opportunity, love and wonderment, and it's meant to be lived to the fullest. Give it everything you've got and have bundles of fun along the way.

I've said it to your brothers, and I'll say it to you. Be thankful you have been born into the greatest country in the world. Never forget how lucky you are to have your freedom. You can dream your dreams and make them come true. Remember that this nation doesn't owe any of us anything. Rather, we all owe the good ol' USA so much, especially our allegiance. Many of us take our country for granted, but people from all over the world know how lucky we are. So many want to come here where they can enjoy unfettered freedom.

There's that word again—freedom. Some people can handle it, and some can't. To certain individuals it means thinking only of themselves and their own gratification. Others are givers. They give all they can to their family, friends and others. They give of their time, talents and energy to help make a better world. They're the ones your grandmother and I respect the most.

As I have grown older, one word keeps coming to mind that I believe spells success or failure in life. That word is attitude. I've watched what a difference the proper attitude can make in peoples' lives. Those who take a positive approach to life are the lucky ones. But we all have to work at it. Sometimes it doesn't come so easily. Some people like to sit around and feel sorry for themselves. They blame their shortcomings and lack of success on others. These doom-and-gloomers focus only on the negative, failing to see opportunity. Emma, be the most enthusiastic and positive person possible. Have a smile on your face as often as you can. Give others the benefit of the doubt, and have a great sense of humor. If you do all these things, people will beat a path to your door.

There is so much I would like to say, but you'll get lots of good advice from your parents, family and friends as you go along. One thing, however, that has helped me as I've gone through life is prayer. Don't be afraid to believe in a higher power. I pray every night for my family, friends and this great nation of ours. It always helps me feel more fulfilled. I bet it will help you, too.

These are just a few of my thoughts, Emma. Nothing too complex, but I did want you to know how happy I am that you're here. We're going to have a lot of adventures together. Frankly, I can't wait.

Miracles happen every day,

Grandpa

IT'S NEVER TOO LATE

Love can come at any age

I remember the phone call as though it were yesterday. It was my mother calling to say she had fallen in love again with a wonderful, romantic man. At the time my mother was 85 and the man she had fallen in love with was 88. They were married soon after. This was my mother's third marriage. She had lost my dad to lung cancer back in 1968, and then a few years ago her second husband also passed away. Her new mate was a great guy, and he just adored my mother. It shows that we can find love again no matter what our age or circumstances if we are open to giving and receiving affection. At least that's my theory. Since true love is so precious and wonderful, I believe stories such as theirs are inspirational.

One of my habits over the years has been to leisurely leaf through the Sunday *New York Times*. One can spend two or three days reading the Sunday editions because they're so extensive. Awhile back I came across a story that caught my attention. It wasn't a big item, but it was something I found both heartwarming and hope-inspiring. It's a love story. Written by Lois Smith Brady, it carried the heading "Vows." The first paragraph reads: "At 72, Clarice K. Olinger is anything but stereotypical. Her hair is naturally black and curly, and she drives very, very fast, zooming up her long driveway like a teen-ager. She runs a mile every day, takes aerobics classes and appears to have none of the usual fears that come with age; neither extra-spicy food nor loneliness concerns her at all.

According to the article, her husband died in 1983, and she continued to live in their large house, which might have spooked a weaker person. Being resolute and independent, she continued living her life to the hilt. Then in the winter of 1990 she attended a singles discussion group in Morristown, N.J. That's where she was introduced to Victor Lindner. It didn't take long for things to get interesting. At 81, Lindner still worked full time as the associate technical director of the Army's Armament Research

Development and Engineering Center in Dover, N.J. There was no grass under his feet. He went windsurfing, canoeing and hiking regularly. Lindner was widowed in 1989. When he met Olinger he had just started dating again, but he hadn't enjoyed much success. According to one of his two daughters, "He'd go out with women, but he said it was very depressing. They'd talk about how they couldn't stand their dead ex-husbands, and that made him nervous."

Soon after meeting Lindner, Olinger took matters into her own hands and made the first move. "I wrote him a postcard and said I'd like to see him again," she said. "I could not phone him. At my age that was not acceptable. It was already a step into the next generation that I even contacted him." Lindner responded almost immediately and invited her to dinner. Then they became a couple on the move. They talked nonstop, jogged together and traveled all over the world. While surrounded by their seven children and her eight grandchildren, they were married in a civil ceremony on the bride's front porch.

There's another interesting side to the story. A number of the bride's children are divorced, and when they witnessed what had happened to their mother, they said it gave them hope. One daughter, Wendy Gray, said: "It made me realize you're never done. You can be at the beginning of your life at all times." That's something too many of us forget because we give up hope and stop living. Olinger and Lindner found each other. Life is too precious to waste on self-pity. Love conquers all.

GONE TO THE DOGS

Opening your heart to your pet is a joyous experience for man and beast

I am a real dog lover but I am also fond of cats, parrots, turtles and just about any other kind of animal. The bond between a pet and a caring owner is so special and wonderful that it is very hard to fully describe. Many people have tried, only to have others poke fun at them for caring so deeply and openly about animals.

I happen to think having a pet to share your love with is almost sacred. What a privilege it is to have that trust and companionship! No matter what your status in life, no matter how bad things get, that pet will always be there for you. A lot of people miss out on this experience and others actively avoid it. To them animals are nuisances; they're unclean, something best kept out of sight and away from people.

I have the opposite belief, that animals make us better people. Of course, having a pet takes love, patience and perseverance, and some people aren't willing to open their hearts to that extent. These people are entitled to their opinion. Not everyone is cut out to be a parent or a pet owner, and I would much rather see them without kids or pets simply because they probably wouldn't do a very good job at either responsibility.

Opening yourself up to an animal carries with it a number of responsibilities, not all of them joyous. The worst is when they pass on. Over the years I've had to put down a number of dogs, including my two loyal and faithful Yorkshire terriers, Pepe and Melissa (who both lived to 18) and then more recently two Alaskan malamutes. The first was Merck, who was 14 when he died. He came into my life in the early 1980s when my son discovered him in the California desert near the Marine base where he was training in desert warfare before heading to the Middle East. Merck was my first experience with a really big dog and when my son went overseas I got to know Merck pretty well. He was a delight. We used to run together; we had more fun than a barrel of monkeys. Unfortunately, there were some times that I remember too well, like the evening we were out running and Merck took great delight in bringing back a big skunk he had captured in the woods. He was sure that I would share in the joy of his conquest.

A couple of months after Merck died, I found Yukon Red up in Fargo, N.D. He was the cutest puppy, and I remember driving him back to Chicago, my wife and I serenading him as we drove along. We fell very much in love with him and enjoyed great adventures with him. Unfortunately, at the age of four he developed stomach cancer and had to be put to sleep.

In each case, as my dog was put to sleep I held it in my arms. Each time it was as if someone had taken my heart away and I couldn't begin to describe the pain and anguish I felt. It was almost unbearable!

But losing Yukon Red didn't stop me. I have another Alaskan malamute named Yodie. He's four years old and just about the best dog you could imagine. We take great walks and love playing together. His personality is different than either Merck or Yukon, but I have been blessed again with a great dog and it gives me so much satisfaction to be his friend. Hopefully, we have a lot of years ahead of us to do all kinds of adventurous things.

That brings me to the real reason for this particular Publisher's Letter. It has to do with a dog named Rocky. He belongs to my assistant of the past 18 years, Cathy Fosco. She's the one who keeps me on the ball, who gets things done when they seem impossible. She is loyal, she is my friend and she is so special that I couldn't possibly fully describe her to you. Suffice it to say she has a heart of gold. When her dad was dying a few years ago, he was in a hospital 25 miles from her home. She was with him every morning and night, tending to his needs, even when he didn't recognize her in the last weeks before he passed away. She did her job as well and was on time every morning.

A few days ago I received a call from Cathy and she was in tears. Her Rocky had gone into acute renal kidney failure and was sinking fast. She was beside herself. I can't chronicle details

of what happened; but she and her husband, Michael, didn't
sleep well for days. They saw all kinds of veterinarians and specialists. They had X-rays taken of Rocky and an ultrasound as
well. As a result, it was discovered that Rocky's kidneys were not
big enough for his 10-pound body.

They were told to put Rocky down. Cathy and her husband
wouldn't hear of it. They eventually had to leave him at a clinic
for three days where he was given intravenous fluids to remove
the toxins that had built up in his body. When they brought him
home he was anything but himself, but each day he gets a little
better and seems to be recovering well with the help of antibi-
otics. The ulcers in his mouth that are typical of renal failure are
disappearing. From absolute despair just a few days ago there is
hope for a little guy who has brought nothing but happiness to
Cathy and Michael. Cathy is smiling now, and she and her husband have gotten a little sleep.

Because of the love of his owners, who refused to listen to the
experts and gave their animal nothing but love and care, it looks
like Rocky may defy the odds and recover. What a great
Christmas present that would be. I'm absolutely convinced that
God does care about all creatures great and small, and Rocky is
one of God's creatures. Joy to the world.

Losing a beloved dog
A heartfelt farewell to Yukon Red

I held him in my arms and told him how much I loved him and always would. I told him he was about the nicest thing that had ever come into my life. He was my best friend, my confidant and my buddy, who gave me unconditional love day in and day out, no matter how I treated him. I couldn't begin to describe how I felt when the veterinarian put four-year-old Yukon Red to sleep. We had shared four years of joy, love and adventures unlike any I've ever had. When I first got him, Red was only seven weeks old but already weighed 14 pounds. A year later he tipped the scale at close to 90 pounds and was probably the handsomest Alaskan malamute you could ever have seen. He was proud, stubborn and affectionate. Every morning when I wasn't traveling we would get up at 4:30 a.m. and meet some of his dog buddies in a nearby town. They would have a terrific time wrestling and running and running and running. Then after about an hour, it was time to go home and chow down. It was a great way to start the day, and watching something you loved having so much fun was the best feeling.

I remember well the circumstances under which I got Red. I had lost my first Alaskan malamute, Merck, and was grieving. It was the summer of 1994, and I had gone up to Detroit Lakes, Minn., where I had a summer place. Merck was a rescue dog my son had found in the Mojave Desert while he was in the Marine Corps and stationed at 29 Palms, Calif. Before my son was put on float with the Third Marine Division for a year, he reluctantly gave Merck to me. Much to my relief when my son returned stateside to go to graduate school, he left Merck with me. Merck, too, was something else. We were very close, and when I had to put him down, I was lost. I couldn't eat; I couldn't sleep; and I was not sure I could go on. I was floundering, but then my wife read in *The Fargo Forum* newspaper a classified ad for Alaskan malamute puppies. Since I had lost Merck only six weeks before that, I told her I wasn't ready for another dog. I said that now we actually had freedom and that I could go with her to Naples, Fla., where she loves to spend the winter. I told her that without taking care of a dog, life would be simpler. Now was the time, I told her, to enjoy our life and our newfound freedom.

Her response was something along these lines: "Without a dog, you'd be lost, and you wouldn't be fun to be around." A short time later we were looking at Alaskan malamute puppies, and Mrs. Lauer picked out Red. When I held him in my arms during the hour-long drive to our summer cabin, I knew we had made the right choice. I named him Yukon Red because when he was a puppy, he was bright red. Later the red turned more brown, but Yukon Red was still something to behold. We were together all the time, and I shared with him my dreams, my fears and thoughts about a variety of subjects. He was the most patient pal you could ever hope for. When we encountered someone, his favorite trick was to roll on his back as if to ask the person to scratch his tummy. To say that people were charmed would be an understatement.

Despite his live-and-let-live nature, he could hold his own. If other dogs tested him, he would growl and stare, and that would usually end the confrontation. He was ominous when challenged, and I thank goodness he had such a good disposition. What a great dog to have as a pet! The end came to Red's young life when, after some X-rays, ultrasounds and other tests, the veterinarian determined that Red had cancer and the disease had spread. Instead of letting him suffer, I put him down almost immediately. I'm still trying to come back from losing him. He'll always be in my heart. Some people say, "It's only a dog." But I can tell you, the richest experience I've ever had is being a dog owner. It has made me a better person. I love you, Red.

When a friend loses a son
A death is a reminder of how valuable it is to keep in close contact

Tom Chapman has always been one of my favorite people. Every time I see him he has a big smile, and we invariably chat for a while and promise we'll keep in closer touch. And then, a long time later, we meet again, and once again promise to stay in contact.

It's tough to keep in touch when everyone is so busy. In fact, it's sad. Some of the nicest people I have ever met I don't really keep in touch with regularly, and yet I think about them from time to time and wonder how they are doing.

Tom and I are lucky in that we're both members of an organization called the Healthcare Research and Development Institute. The group includes about 40 of the top healthcare chief executive officers in the country and some corporate members. Corporate members use this unique forum to find out what this select group of CEOs is thinking about. This helps *Modern Healthcare* do a better job of serving our readers.

Tom is considered one of best and brightest healthcare executives in the industry, and consequently when we get together, I'm always interested in what he has to say. Tom is president and CEO of the HSC Foundation in Washington. The foundation's mission is to facilitate access to appropriate care and services for children with special needs and their families in the Washington metropolitan area. It also works on regional and national projects with governmental, private and philanthropic organizations to serve the same population. Tom has held a number of top healthcare positions, running George Washington University Medical Center and Greater Southeast Healthcare System, both in Washington. Needless to say, he knows his stuff and is well-respected for it.

I am writing about Tom because of a tragedy that befell his family: the death of his son, Darrian Chapman, who suffered a heart attack at the tender age of 37.

The younger Chapman had been a television sports reporter

in Washington for five years before coming to Chicago as a sports anchor at WMAQ, the local NBC affiliate, in 2000. He had suffered a heart attack in 1997, but despite his health problems he was an avid participant in sports, particularly hockey and golf. In fact, he suffered his fatal heart attack at a hockey rink in Chicago.

Darrian in a short time had become a fixture in the sports scene in Chicago. He was an enthusiastic sportsman, and viewers were charmed by his positive outlook.

Upon hearing the news of Darrian's death, I was saddened for him and his family, but frankly I didn't know he was Tom's son until I talked to Diane Appleyard, president and CEO of HRDL. When I found out, I didn't know what to do. What do you say to a man who has lost a son? What could you possibly say to give him comfort?

I did call him, even though by that time the memorial services already had taken place. I learned long ago that in a time of tragedy too many of us are embarrassed to call someone in the midst of his or her sorrow. But I talked to Tom and told him how sorry I was and we talked things through. I believe it helped him and I know it helped me. I asked him to send me some of the clippings and remembrances from Darrian's memorial service in Chicago.

The things that were said were what you would expect about an exuberant, talented, enthusiastic person who loved his work, his friends and his family. His pastor, in the eulogy for Darrian, quoted the young man's philosophy on life: "As he once said, 'It's not the destination that counts, it's the journey.' And what a journey Darrian Chapman had. He loved life. He loved his family. He loved (his wife) Debbie. He loved his children, Marissa and Jordan. He loved his job. He loved Chicago. He loved his sports. He loved food. He loved his church. He loved God."

Darrian's grandfather, Mark Battle, spoke on behalf of the family and described Darrian. "He was a giver. That is to say, he literally gave himself to life and the causes he adopted. His giving was a personal contribution of self, beyond dollars and cents. Ask anyone who knew him close-up and you will find his gifts were priceless."

Larry Wert, Darrian's boss at WMAQ, offered this: "We received hundreds and hundreds of e-mails (after Darrian's death), and I've pulled some of the most frequently repeated words writers used to describe Darrian: warm, friendly, passionate, charismatic, trustworthy, genuine, competitive, affable, loud, caring, honest, proud. But most of all, real."

Here is what I have to say to Tom: The apple doesn't fall far from the tree, and from what I have read about your son, he was very much like you, always giving and taking joy in doing so. You have given this great industry everything you have through your devotion, love and intellect. Thank goodness for the commitment you have made to all of us and thank goodness your son lived such a full life in so short a time. If I were to describe the Tom Chapman I have known over the years, the words Darrian's boss used to describe him are the same ones I would use to describe you. All of us send our prayers and love to you and Darrian's family.

THE LESSONS WE HAVE LEARNED

A year later, we can see the lasting changes of 9-11 in our country and our lives

I was asked recently if America had changed in the year since the terrorist attacks of Sept. 11. I had to think about it for a while, because it's a complex question. But looking back on all that has happened, I do think we have emerged from this experience a better country.

Our government certainly has changed. We're on a war footing, and this fight to end terrorism is going to take some time to win. I think we as a people have changed in that most of us have awakened to the fact that our way of life is under fire and that there are people all over the world who would like to see this great nation humiliated and destroyed. I have been impressed by the reaction of so many young people, who have rallied to the cause, especially those who volunteer to serve in the armed forces. I'm in awe of their love of country, their willingness to sacrifice for the common good of the nation. There was a time when I wondered if this country was ever threatened or invaded by another hostile force, would we have the resolve to defend ourselves? I thought we had become too soft. I was wrong.

We see smaller changes in the way we live. We seem to understand that being with our loved ones is the most important part of our lives. We are kissing more and hugging more with our family members as well as our friends and acquaintances.

I also am impressed by the goodness and generosity of the people in this country who continue to give their time, energy and money to so many worthwhile causes, especially the Sept. 11 relief funds. Even as the fires at the World Trade Center and Pentagon were still burning, we came together as one nation with our outpouring of caring. Race didn't matter. Religion didn't matter. If a victim came from another country, that didn't matter either. What did matter to Americans was that other people had been devastated by the events of 9-11. People needed help and others sent clothing, money, food and other vitally important items. It was one of this country's most tragic hours, but also one of its finest.

Then there were the leaders who came forward— who can forget them?—Mayor Rudy Giuliani standing at the microphones looking exhausted but giving the press concise, up-to-date information about a tragedy that only hours before had nearly claimed him as a victim. This was a man who just days before had been reeling from his messy divorce and prostate cancer. Nobody could have predicted that he soon would be viewed as a national hero and would have been elected to another term if the law had allowed it.

President Bush surprised a lot of people as well by his demeanor and resolve. Many didn't think he had it in him. His State of the Union address may go down as one of the defining moments in American history Then there's Secretary of Defense Donald Rumsfeld. Who isn't impressed by his grasp of the facts and his candor at press briefings? True leaders emerge in difficult times to help bring reason and perspective to chaotic situations and make things right.

But it was the more ordinary people who may have made the biggest difference. I still can't believe the courage and dedication of those firefighters and police officers, who didn't hesitate one moment before going into the horrific, nightmarish scenes in those buildings to rescue their fellow citizens. They knew they might not come out alive. Many never did. Now, we look at all public servants differently. We realize that we have people risking their lives every day to keep us safer. The problem is, we don't pay them anything close to what they deserve.

The same is true of nurses. We need them, but we don't pay them very much. When someone leaves a hospital, often they judge the care they received by the attention they received from nurses, not physicians. Too often, however, nurses are taken for granted. One young lady I know is an operating room nurse in Milwaukee. She is a veteran and is well-trained, but she only makes about $40,000 a year when she could work for a drug company and make far more. Pay isn't the only issue. Nurses generally are not treated well by doctors and administrators, who consider them a part of the overhead.

The drama of Sept. 11 keeps coming back to me in vivid detail. I remember calling David Campbell, the CEO of the parent of Saint Vincent's Hospital and Medical Center, which is near the World Trade Center. It was the day after the tragedy and I wanted him to know I cared about what was happening. Our conversation was to the point: "How are you doing?" "I'm OK and we are ready to go, but there are no (victims) coming in." At that time we all hoped there would be survivors but unfortunately there weren't many even though Saint Vincent's and other surrounding healthcare facilities were ready for them. And who can forget the dedication of the nurses and physicians who went to ground zero?

I wrote a while back about a young woman who was pulled out of the World Trade Center and rushed to NYU Downtown Hospital. It was thought that in order to save her life one of her legs would have to be amputated. As a team of physicians huddled over the young woman an orthopedic physician asked for a chance to save her leg, and he did through some absolutely fantastic surgery. This past spring she got married, and saved the first dance at the reception for the young doctor. Out of tragic circumstances often come hope and inspiration.

Now we are at war, sending our gallant young people into harm's way in far-flung places. Most of us have suddenly awakened to the fact that there are people in this world who hate and despise us because of our lifestyle and freedom. Knowing that has to change how any of us looks at the world. Maybe the time has come for all of us to realize that freedom and liberty don't come cheap. That might be the biggest change of all. None of us will ever be the same.

One canadian's tribute
Gordon Sinclair stands up for the U.S.

The luckiest thing that ever happened to me was to be born a citizen of the United States of America. I've always been very proud of my country. Today, however, if someone expresses love for this great nation of ours, the cynics and elitists will say that the person is simply ignorant of all the injustices and inequities that are part of our society. But there are plenty of people who are objective about what we are as a nation, and some of the things they say should make all of us proud.

One such person was a Canadian TV commentator who passed away a number of years ago. Gordon Sinclair was an out-spoken individual, and according to a good friend of mine from Toronto, when Sinclair got his dander up, he really spoke from the heart. You could even say he was Canada's version of Paul Harvey. Someone recently sent me an article about Sinclair, and I thought I would share some of the comments he made on one of his shows a number of years ago after hearing certain individuals attack the good old U.S.A. The following are excerpts from a Canadian newspaper:

"This Canadian thinks it is time to speak up for the Americans as the most generous and possibly the least-appreciated people on the earth.

"Germany, Japan and, to a lesser extent, Britain and Italy were lifted out of the debris of war by the Americans who poured in billions of dollars and forgave others billions in debts. When France was in danger of collapsing in 1956, it was the Americans who propped it up, and their reward was to be insulted and swindled on the streets of Paris. I was there. I saw it.

"When earthquakes hit distant cities, it is the United States that hurries in to help, The Marshall Plan and the Truman Policy pumped billions of dollars into discouraged countries. Now newspapers in those countries write about the decadent, war-mongering Americans. When the railways of France, Germany and India were breaking down because of age, it was the

Americans who rebuilt them.

"You talk about scandals, and the Americans put theirs right in the store window for everybody to look at.

"I can name 5,000 times when the Americans raced to the help of other people in trouble. Can you name me even one time when someone else raced to the Americans in trouble? Our neighbors have faced it alone, and I'm one Canadian who is damned tired of hearing them get kicked around. Stand proud, America!"

Those are a few thoughts from a Canadian, some years ago, but his message stands the test of time. America has done a lot of things right over the years. We should keep his reflections in mind as we go about our business every day. It's especially important in this age of global economics and interdependence. Maybe some of our old and new partners would do well to remember the model of generosity this nation and its citizens have always displayed when others needed help. We are blessed.